In Fragile Moments & *The Last Time*

THE AZRIELI SERIES OF HOLOCAUST SURVIVOR MEMOIRS:
PUBLISHED TITLES

ENGLISH TITLES

In Fragile Moments
Zsuzsanna Fischer Spiro

The Last Time
Eva Shainblum

THE AZRIELI FOUNDATION
www.azrielifoundation.org

Cover and book design by Mark Goldstein
Endpaper maps by Martin Gilbert
Map on page xxxv by François Blanc
Translation of Zsuzsanna Fischer Spiro's diary excerpts on pages 20–27 and 36–42
by Marietta Morry and Lynda Muir

LIBRARY AND ARCHIVES CANADA CATALOGUING IN PUBLICATION

In fragile moments / Zsuzsanna Fischer Spiro.
    The last time / Eva Shainblum.

(The Azrieli series of Holocaust survivor memoirs)
Includes index.
ISBN 978-1-988065-03-8 (paperback)

1. Fischer Spiro, Zsuzsanna, 1925–. 2. Shainblum, Eva, 1927–. 3. Holocaust, Jewish
(1939–1945) – Hungary – Personal narratives. 4. Holocaust survivors – Hungary –
Biography. 5. Holocaust, Jewish (1939–1945). 6. World War, 1939–1945 – Concentration camps. I. Fischer Spiro, Zsuzsanna, 1925– . In fragile moments. II. Shainblum,
Eva, 1927– . Last time. III. Azrieli Foundation issuing body IV. Title: Last time.

DS135.H93A18 2016   940.53'180922439   C2016-902254-4

PRINTED IN CANADA

The Azrieli Series of Holocaust Survivor Memoirs

Naomi Azrieli, Publisher

Jody Spiegel, Program Director
Arielle Berger, Managing Editor
Farla Klaiman, Editor
Elizabeth Lasserre, Senior Editor, French-Language Editions
Elin Beaumont, Senior Educational Outreach and Events Coordinator
Catherine Person, Educational Outreach and Events Coordinator,
    Quebec and French Canada
Marc-Olivier Cloutier, Educational Outreach and Events Assistant,
    Quebec and French Canada
Tim MacKay, Digital Platform Manager
Elizabeth Banks, Digital Asset and Curator Archivist
Susan Roitman, Office Manager (Toronto)
Mary Mellas, Executive Assistant and Human Resources (Montreal)

Mark Goldstein, Art Director
François Blanc, Cartographer
Bruno Paradis, Layout, French-Language Editions

Contents

Series Preface:
In their own words...

In telling these stories, the writers have liberated themselves. For so many years we did not speak about it, even when we became free people living in a free society. Now, when at last we are writing about what happened to us in this dark period of history, knowing that our stories will be read and live on, it is possible for us to feel truly free. These unique historical documents put a face on what was lost, and allow readers to grasp the enormity of what happened to six million Jews – one story at a time.

David J. Azrieli, C.M., C.Q., M.Arch
Holocaust survivor and founder, The Azrieli Foundation

Since the end of World War II, over 30,000 Jewish Holocaust survivors have immigrated to Canada. Who they are, where they came from, what they experienced and how they built new lives for themselves and their families are important parts of our Canadian heritage. The Azrieli Foundation's Holocaust Survivor Memoirs Program was established to preserve and share the memoirs written by those who survived the twentieth-century Nazi genocide of the Jews of Europe and later made their way to Canada. The program is guided by the conviction that each survivor of the Holocaust has a remarkable story to tell, and that such stories play an important role in education about tolerance and diversity.

Millions of individual stories are lost to us forever. By preserving the stories written by survivors and making them widely available to a broad audience, the Azrieli Foundation's Holocaust Survivor Memoirs Program seeks to sustain the memory of all those who perished at the hands of hatred, abetted by indifference and apathy. The personal accounts of those who survived against all odds are as different as the people who wrote them, but all demonstrate the courage, strength, wit and luck that it took to prevail and survive in such terrible adversity. The memoirs are also moving tributes to people – strangers and friends – who risked their lives to help others, and who, through acts of kindness and decency in the darkest of moments, frequently helped the persecuted maintain faith in humanity and courage to endure. These accounts offer inspiration to all, as does the survivors' desire to share their experiences so that new generations can learn from them.

The Holocaust Survivor Memoirs Program collects, archives and publishes these distinctive records and the print editions are available free of charge to educational institutions and Holocaust-education programs across Canada. They are also available for sale to the general public at bookstores. All revenues to the Azrieli Foundation from the sales of the Azrieli Series of Holocaust Survivor Memoirs go toward the publishing and educational work of the memoirs program.

$$\sim$$

The Azrieli Foundation would like to express appreciation to the following people for their invaluable efforts in producing this book: Doris Bergen, Sherry Dodson (Maracle Press), Helen Guri, Barbara Kamieński, Marietta Morry, Lynda Muir, Therese Parent, Fran Weisman, and Margie Wolfe & Emma Rodgers of Second Story Press.

About the Glossary

The following memoir contains a number of terms, concepts and historical references that may be unfamiliar to the reader. For information on major organizations; significant historical events and people; geographical locations; religious and cultural terms; and foreign-language words and expressions that will help give context and background to the events described in the text, please see the glossary beginning on page 95.

Introduction

This volume features the testimonies of two survivors of the Holocaust in Hungary and of deportation to Auschwitz: Zsuzsanna Fischer Spiro and Eva Shainblum. Today, over seventy years after the liberation of Auschwitz, as the last survivor witnesses are disappearing, it is particularly urgent to preserve the voices of as many of them as possible. In framing history through these personal experiences, it becomes possible to piece together a partial collective autobiography of the victims of the Holocaust. The power of these first-person accounts is not primarily that they increase concrete knowledge of larger historical events, but that they provide a picture of how daily life was lived and then suddenly transformed in a flash, of the Jewish culture that was wiped out during the Holocaust, along with its victims. In the accounts of concentration camp survivors, as opposed to those who survived in hiding, we find many recurring details, because every individual testimony documents a collective fact in a "unity of misery," and yet each one preserves its own unique character within those details.[1]

European Jews experienced the Holocaust in many different

---

1 On the concept of the "unity of misery," see Terrence Des Pres, *The Survivor: An Anatomy of Life in the Death Camps* (Oxford: Oxford UP, 1976) and Geoffrey Hartman, *The Longest Shadow: In the Aftermath of the Holocaust* (Bloomington: Indiana UP, 1996, 34).

ways; gender, age, social status, religiosity, time and geographic loca-
tion were of great importance. The situation of Hungarian Jews was
unique in a number of ways, with the Holocaust coming in the last
part of the war, when most of the Jews of Europe had already been
annihilated and when it was clear that Nazi Germany would lose the
war. The Hungarian Holocaust was nevertheless characterized by its
speed and intensity, making it the most efficient mass murder cam-
paign of the war.

Historically, Hungarian Jews were among the most acculturated
in Eastern Europe. Having been granted citizenship and civil rights
under the Habsburg Dual Monarchy, both secular and religious Jews
saw themselves as patriots, and most of them preferred to speak
Hungarian rather than Yiddish. With the dissolution of the Austro-
Hungarian Empire after World War 1, Hungary lost two-thirds of
its territory and three-fifths of its population in the 1920 Treaty of
Trianon. With the country thus shorn of most of its former ethnic
groups, the Jews were left as the most vulnerable minority.

From 1933, in the hope of regaining its lost territories, Hungary
closely collaborated in its foreign policy with Nazi Germany. Between
1938 and 1941, through that collaboration and due to Western appease-
ment of Germany, Hungary regained parts of Slovakia, Transylvania
and what are today Serbia and Croatia. The re-annexation of lost territories added two and a half million people, significantly increasing
the Jewish minority as well as the population of foreign Jews from
occupied Eastern Europe, who had escaped to then still independent
Hungary.

Throughout the late 1930s and early 1940s, in the context of eupho-
ria following the reclamation of some of the lost territories, Hungary
introduced increasingly restrictive antisemitic legislation with the
aim of excluding Jews from the political, social and economic life of
the country. In June 1941, spurred by the desire for further territory –
which could be achieved only through alliances with the Third Reich
– Hungary entered the war as an independent ally of Germany. From
then on, antisemitic legislation as well as violence against Jews fur-

ther intensified, culminating in their legal exclusion from Hungarian society, as well as in two large-scale massacres.

The first massacre occurred shortly after Hungary entered the war, when, beginning in mid-July 1941 and continuing through August, the Hungarian gendarmerie and military proceeded to deport to certain death tens of thousands of Jews from Subcarpathia. Some had been born in Hungary but were either unable to prove their citizenship or simply caught up in the mass chaos. Others were refugees, mostly from Poland and Russia but also from Western countries. Although the actual murders of over 23,000 people were carried out across the border in Kamenets-Podolsk by Germans and their Ukrainian accomplices, the massacres could not have taken place without the complicity of the Hungarian authorities, who delivered the victims to the Germans.

In 1942, German and Hungarian troops committed more massacres in the reclaimed "Southern Territories" of Vojvodina (Délvidék and Újvidék), using partisan activity in the area as an excuse to kill thousands of Serbs and some seven hundred Jews.[2] In addition, from the beginning of the war, Jewish men of military age had been conscripted into the increasingly brutal forced labour battalions, or *Munkaszolgálat*, under the auspices of the Hungarian army. The conditions in these units became the cause of the majority of Jewish deaths prior to the German occupation. Some conscripts died of starvation or typhus or froze to death, while others were murdered outright by elements of the Hungarian army and gendarmerie or fell into Soviet captivity.[3]

Paradoxically, in early 1944, in the fifth year of World War II, there were still over 800,000 Jews in Hungary (including some 100,000 converts identified as Jews under the racial laws), living in what they

---

2 Randolph Braham, "The Kamenets Podolsk and Délvidék Massacres: Prelude to the Holocaust in Hungary." *Yad Vashem Studies* 9 (1973): 133–156.

3 Robert Rozett, *Conscripted Slaves. Hungarian Forced Laborers on the Eastern Front During the Second World War* (Jerusalem: Yad Vashem, 2014).

thought was relative physical protection. On March 19, 1944, Hitler, prompted by concerns that Admiral Horthy was trying to extricate the country from the war, occupied its ally, sending a small group of SS under the command of Adolf Eichmann. This was the start of the rapid implementation of the Holocaust in Hungary, which, however, was made possible only by collaboration and active initiative on the part of some 200,000 Hungarians, ranging from radically antisemitic officials, to gendarmes, to local civilians. The Nazi occupation allowed these Hungarians to fully achieve their long-term goals of pillaging Jewish property and appropriating Jewish businesses, a process that had been legally developing in the country since 1938. The process of destruction followed quickly, with a continuum of further restrictions: by the beginning of April, all Jews over the age of six were ordered to wear the yellow star, and all valuables were confiscated; on April 28, ghettos in provincial Hungary were established. On May 15, not even a full two months after the occupation, systematic deportations from the provinces began, almost all to Auschwitz-Birkenau. In all, 437,402 Hungarian Jews were deported in daily transports within a mere fifty-six days; the great majority of them were murdered on arrival.

Up until the spring of 1944, Treblinka, Bełżec and Sobibór had been the main centres of Nazi killing. It was not until the arrival of the Hungarian Jewish transports that Auschwitz-Birkenau became the epicentre of the Final Solution and the site of the largest mass murder, with hundreds of thousands of Hungarian Jews killed there. By the end of the war, more than half a million Hungarian Jews would be killed in ghettos, boxcars, Lagers and the forced labour service, or shot into the Danube River.[4]

---

4 Randolph L. Braham, "Foreword." (*The Nazis' Last Victims: The Holocaust in Hungary.* Randolph L. Braham, with Scott Miller, eds. Detroit: Wayne State UP, 1998) and Zoltán Vági, László Csősz and Gábor Kádár, *The Holocaust in Hungary: Evolution of a Genocide* (Lanham: AltaMira Press, 2013). For a brief overview, see Kinga

~

Zsuzsanna Fischer Spiro was the third of four children of Orthodox parents, born in 1925 in the small village of Tornyospálca (present-day population: about 2,000), located in Szabolcs-Szatmár-Bereg county in the Northeastern Great Plains region of Hungary. In her nostalgic reminiscence, she recalls a happy childhood in the "peaceful" village with no paved roads or any modern conveniences, although her family's house had electricity, a big luxury at the time, and they also had the first and only radio in the village. While the Jewish children went to public school with Christian children and she had non-Jewish friends, she adds that "we weren't so close" and, being kosher, she could not eat anything in their homes. Although she was from a religious family, the fact that she attended public school was not unusual; in pre-war Subcarpathia the public schools were either Catholic or Protestant, and Jews were required by law to attend one or the other. In spite of recalling a peaceful life, she does recount that at one point all the Jewish students in the village who had attended the Catholic school were transferred to the Protestant school because the Catholic priest was antisemitic and had told his congregation that the Jews had killed Jesus. Given her comment that, at the time, she didn't even know who Jesus was, the anecdote illustrates not only the antisemitism smouldering just under the surface but also the extreme social isolation in which religious Jews lived. In Tornyospálca there were only fifteen to twenty Jewish families, numbering some fifty souls, all of whom would be deported. In 1963, the synagogue was torn down, and today there are no Jews remaining in the village.

In 1937, Zsuzsanna's family moved to Kisvárda, the market centre of the surrounding agricultural region, located twelve kilometres

---

Frojimovics, "The Special Characteristics of the Holocaust in Hungary, 1938–45." *History of the Holocaust* (New York: Routledge, 2010).

from Tornyospálca. Near the present border of Slovakia and Ukraine, Kisvárda is a town that, even during the interwar period of border changes, always belonged to Hungary. By the early 1800s, many Jews lived in Kisvárda and its area, and most spoke Hungarian rather than Yiddish, as they primarily identified themselves as Hungarian. By 1937, Kisvárda had a large Jewish community, representing about 30 per cent of the population, with a substantial community of ultra-Orthodox; it had so many Jewish stores that few were open on the Sabbath.[5]

Zsuzsanna mentions that by 1940 she began to hear from Jewish refugees from Poland about the persecution, but not about the killings there. Her comment illustrates one of the most important characteristics of the belatedness of the Holocaust in Hungary, in terms of what the Jews of Hungary could know at the time, or what they were capable of believing about what the genocide unfolding around them meant for their future. Both her father and her twenty-one-year-old brother were conscripted into the *Munkaszolgálat*. Although Zsuzsanna briefly describes the virulently antisemitic atmosphere between 1940 and 1944, when new anti-Jewish laws were being constantly passed, Jewish property pillaged and Jews insulted and scapegoated, her narrative focuses on March 19, 1944, when the Germans occupied Hungary and immediately passed more anti-Jewish laws. When Jews were ordered to wear a yellow star, she didn't go out of the house for days because she felt so violated.

In the Kisvárda ghetto, where all Jews from the surrounding area were forced to live, some 7,000 Jews were confined to the Jewish quarter around the synagogue. Approximately half of the ghetto inhabitants were locals, with the rest gathered from the surrounding villages. Deportations from Hungary started on May 15, and the

---

5   See further the web page by Peter Spiro, Zsuzsanna's son, on his family's history in the area at www.peterspiro.com/spirofam.htm

Kisvárda ghetto was evacuated in two transports, on May 29 and May 31, with Zsuzsanna and her family in the second transport. By June 5, 1944, the Deputy Prefect was able to announce that Szabolcs county was now *judenfrei*, free of Jews. That is, by June 1944, with incredible efficiency, Hungary had been emptied of its rural Jewish population, 95 per cent of whom were to be killed.[6]

Zsuzsanna testifies to how the Hungarian gendarmes carried out the ghettoization and deportation, specifically recalling that the first time she ever saw a German officer was long after the whole ghettoization process had been completed by the Hungarians, and only a few days before the deportation to Auschwitz. She also recalls that Hungarians who watched them walk to the railway station were laughing as they went by. Besides describing the appalling thirst and crowding of those forced to wait for hours for the train and then being shoved onto hideously overcrowded boxcars – humiliating conditions that we have come to know from many accounts – she talks about how the most important concern for her family was to stay together, as they had no inkling of how soon they would be parted forever. In a further irony, she recalls their train arriving in Auschwitz on June 2, on a Friday night, which called up a vision of her past life, when her mother would light the Shabbat candles. Instead of candles glowing, though, they saw flames shooting out of a chimney, accompanied by a terrible smell they could not identify.

As Imre Kertész wrote in his autobiographical novel *Fatelessness*, his first days in the camp engraved themselves in his memory far more than anything that happened later, which is natural for people whose lives and very identities are suddenly transformed overnight into those of prisoners. In this context, it is natural that Zsuzsanna's

---

6   See Randolph Braham, *The Politics of Genocide. The Holocaust in Hungary* (Detroit: Wayne State UP, 2000: 121) and Tim Cole, *Traces of the Holocaust: Journeying In and Out of the Ghettos* (New York: Continuum, 2011: 30–33).

narrative about Auschwitz also focuses on the oft-repeated horror scenes of arrival, separation from family members and the gamut of deliberate humiliations, sexual exposure and ridicule in front of leering SS men, including the forced nude showers, delousing and shaving of hair, all much more harrowing for religious young women, many of whom had never even seen their own mothers in the nude. Prisoners had to surrender all their clothing, including underwear, and female prisoners were initially issued not prison uniforms but only random leftover rags not suitable for sending to Germany – rags which, as Zsuzsanna recalls, in her case were an evening gown and a pair of men's shorts for underwear. She never again saw her own outfit, which had been her favourite, since, as did so many others, she had dressed in her best clothes for the trip.

Zsuzsanna was lucky to be selected along with her sister; this was the key to their eventual survival. Despite undergoing constant selections, they had several miraculous escapes from what they most feared: one of them being selected, a scene they were forced to witness many times with other sisters. She recounts how happy they were to meet a cousin who was there with her three sisters. All of them tried to help each other, which illustrates the common thread of relationships and bonding in women's memoirs: typically, two or three women would create a camp sisterhood, striving to keep each other alive. As Isabella Leitner, another deportee from Kisvárda, wrote in her memoir, "If you are sisterless, you do not have the pressure, the absolute responsibility to end the day alive" (59).[7]

---

7   See the memoir of Isabella Katz Leitner, *Fragments of Isabella* (New York: Crowell, 1978). Born in 1924, one year before Zsuzsanna, Isabella was also deported from the Kisvárda ghetto with her four sisters, brother and mother. She recalls that they started the journey on May 29 and arrived in Auschwitz on May 31; she also recounts that they left Kisvárda to the cheers of former neighbours. Compare as well the short testimony of Veronika Schwartz, born in 1927, who was also deported from the Kisvárda ghetto, available online at migs.concordia.ca/mem-

Before Zsuzsanna and her sister were sent off on a slave labour transport to Germany in October 1944 they were tattooed, and she expresses the horror she felt at this loss of identity with the words, "I cannot describe what it was like to become a nameless slave." Interestingly, this passage indicates that they were among those who were not tattooed on arrival at Auschwitz; in the summer of 1944, with the arrival of excessively large Hungarian transports, the tattooing system broke down for lack of ink.[8]

The two sisters arrived in Markkleeberg, near Leipzig, where, as she recounts, the barracks were luxurious in comparison to those in Auschwitz: a single bed with a blanket for every person, more food and actual grey uniforms. In other ways, however, with barbed wire and guards, it was a miniature Auschwitz. Where they had arrived as slave labourers was the Junkers aircraft factory in Leipzig, an important centre for the German Luftwaffe in World War II, that produced the so-called *Schnellbomber*, fast bombers, one of the Luftwaffe's most effective aerial weapons and an integral part of the *Blitzkrieg*, lightning war, strategy. The sisters were part of a group of 1,300 Hungarian women slave labourers from Hungary and annexed Hungarian territories leased out by the SS to Junkers. They arrived in four transports: the first transport of 500 arrived on August 31, 1944; the second and third on October 15 and 25, with 200 and 300 women, respectively, and a final transport of 300 on December 8.

Zsuzsanna and her sister must have been in the first of the October

---

oirs/vschwartz/vschwartz.html as part of volume 15 of the memoirs of Holocaust Survivors in Canada. The project was initiated in the early 1990s by faculty of the Canadian Jewish Studies Department of Concordia University of Montreal, which set out to collect unpublished memoirs of Holocaust survivors living in Canada. 43–58.

8 Cf. another survivor, Iby Knill, for whom the distinction of not having been tattooed was such a marker of identity that she entitled her memoir *The Woman Without a Number* (Leeds: Scratching Shed Pub., 2010).

transports, since she refers to the food situation deteriorating with the arrival of later transports. Sometimes the women prisoners were forced to do hard and dangerous work, such as carrying heavy stones, as Zsuzsanna recalls, although she could no longer remember for what purpose. However, later she worked on delicate machinery, recounting that at one point she had to work on a very special machine, of which there were only two in the factory. Zsuzsanna's account is corroborated by a recent study by Daniel Uziel, who relates that the inmates in the Junkers factory were Hungarian schoolgirls and housewives who arrived in 1944 – arguably the most unskilled workforce possible – and yet were quickly trained in drilling, filling, riveting and other specialized skills.[9]

A memoir and historical study by fellow Hungarian Zahava Szász Stessel sheds further light on the female slave labour experiences described by Zsuzsanna.[10] Zahava was only fourteen when she and her younger sister were sent from Hungary and through Auschwitz to work in Markkleeberg. While Zahava tells her own story, which is much like that of Zsuzsanna and includes work at the stone quarry and the forced death march following the evacuation of the camp, she also consulted all the other surviving Hungarian women she could find in order to compare their memories; she also scoured extant records, so that she offers an extraordinarily detailed record of camp life, along with blueprints and lists of inmates. She recounts anecdotes, such as that the new arrivals would be greeted in Hungarian

---

9 Daniel Uziel, *Arming the Luftwaffe: The German Aviation Industry in World War II* (Jefferson, NC: McFarland and Co., 2011: 221).

10 Zahava Szász Stessel, *Snow Flowers: Hungarian Jewish Women in an Airplane Factory* (Madison, NJ: Fairleigh Dickinson UP, 2009): 58. See also Erzsébet Frank, *365 Nap [365 Days]* (Budapest: Uránus, 1996, original edition, 1946), a memoir in poetry of her deportation, long sections of which she composed on scraps of paper in Markkleeberg and read to her fellow inmates there.

by girls from various cities and towns in Hungary, telling them that they had arrived in a better camp. One example of the kind of detail Zahava is able to recreate from the composite recollections of her *sorstársak*, companions in distress, is the description of the prison uniform that they were issued, "of dark gray cotton overalls made from hard, thin, canvas-like materials, a shirt to wear underneath … on the side of the pants was a red stripe and a large red X painted in oil on the back of the blouse … to identify them as prisoners." On the later death march, these prison uniforms were to become a real hindrance, as they were identifiable by the German population.

Another detail that Zsuzsanna mentions about camp life in Markkleeberg is that when the women weren't working, one of their favourite pastimes was to exchange recipes, an activity that she didn't engage in and didn't even like to listen to. She surmised that maybe the others thought it would help them forget how hungry they were. As I discuss in more detail elsewhere, food talk was a survival tool to recall the women's past lives and to counteract the stripping of their gender identity and dehumanization.[11] Compare Ruth Klüger, aged fourteen when in the camp, who recalls that adult women engaged in food talk, dubbed "cooking with the mouth," much as she herself recited poems:

> At night a favourite game was to surpass each other
> with the recital of
> generous amounts of butter, eggs, and sugar in fan-
> tasy baking contests.
> I didn't even know many of the dishes they cooked

---

11 Louise O. Vasvári, "En-gendering Memory Through Alimentary Life Writing of the Holocaust." CLCweb *Special Issue: Life Writing and the Trauma of War* 17.3 (2015).

and listened with a
growling stomach, just as I listened with a hungry
imagination to their
tales of travel, parties, dates, and university studies.[12]

By the beginning of April, the inmates in Markkleeberg noticed that the German guards were beginning to act strangely, and though the end was near, they forced the prisoners to embark on a final death march. Zsuzsanna describes in excruciating detail the endless marching for some two weeks, sometimes seemingly in circles, clothed only in those factory uniforms and without shoes, with no food other than the occasional raw potato they might find in a field, and forced to beg and steal along the way. They were finally liberated on May 8, 1945, and managed to arrive back in Hungary a month later, where, as she saw the border, she was ashamed to admit that she was "homesick for the country that had treated [her] so badly." Although so many of her relatives "never came back," in Budapest she found that her grandmother and aunt had survived, and a short time later her father and one brother also appeared. Most of the other young survivors left, but her family decided to stay, moving back to their looted home and trying to start life anew.

At the conclusion of her testimony, Zsuzsanna divulges that near the end of the war she was able to write down her immediate memories of what she had experienced and that on the basis of that diary, twenty years later, in 1976, she typed out her story in both Hungarian and English for her family. Now, another forty years later, her memories appear here for a broader public.

∼

---

12 Ruth Klüger, *Still Alive: A Holocaust Girlhood Remembered* (New York: The Feminist Press, 2001: 117).

Eva Shainblum, born (in 1927) two years after Zsuzsanna Spiro and less than two hundred kilometres away from her, came from a very similar background. Her family lived in the small city of Oradea, in northwestern Romania; the town's Hungarian name is Nagyvárad and its German name Grosswardein. The names were used during different historical periods depending on who ruled the area – better known in the Western world as Transylvania. At the end of World War I, under the Treaty of Trianon, Transylvania was awarded to the Kingdom of Romania and remained under its rule until August 30, 1940, when it was re-annexed to Hungary. The mass of celebrators, including Hungarian-speaking Jews like Eva's father, welcomed the Hungarians. Following the defeat of Nazi Germany, Northern Transylvania, including Nagyvárad, again became part of Romania.

The first synagogue in Nagyvárad/Oradea was erected in 1803 and the first school in 1839. The Jewish community was divided primarily between an overwhelming majority of Orthodox denominations, including Hassidim, and a smaller number of Neolog or modern Conservative congregations, although the city was also a centre of Jewish liberalism. In the early part of the twentieth century, much like in Budapest, many Jews rose to prominence in public life, although at the same time a great proportion remained poor, especially in the northwestern parts, which were inhabited by large numbers of Yiddish-speaking Orthodox who resisted modernization.

With the re-annexation of the area to Hungary, the fate of Transylvanian Jews, who had adopted the Hungarian language and culture, became entwined with the fate of Hungarian Jews. Aside from the Budapest ghetto, the largest ghetto in Trianon Hungary was set up in Nagyvárad and actually consisted of two ghettos: the first for the city's some 27,000 Jews, the second with nearly 8,000 from the surrounding rural communities. The terribly overpopulated ghettos were liquidated in nine transports between May 23 and June

3.[13] About 2,000 survivors returned and, after the war, when the area once again belonged to Romania, most left during later periods of legal emigration. Today, only a few hundred Jews remain, who form a functioning community.[14]

Like Zsuzsanna, Eva also recalls a happy family life, a culture, later erased, with special attention given to the description of Jewish holidays, with delicious meals as the means of transmitting Jewish customs and heritage, rather than specific religious observance. She emphasizes that her family spoke Hungarian and not Yiddish at home, as both of her parents were fluent in Hungarian. In school, even after the Romanians took over Nagyvárad and changed the name of the city to Oradea, the teachers continued to teach in Hungarian. Oradea had a full Jewish cultural life in the entire spectrum of Jewish denominations, as well as all sorts of political groups, including Zionist youth groups and theatres, where Jewish theatre groups from not only Budapest and Bucharest but also Poland performed.

Although Eva and her family heard stories in the mid-1930s of rising antisemitic activity, as a sheltered child in a Jewish neighbour-

---

13 Randolph L. Braham. *Genocide and Retribution* (The Hague: Kluwer, 1983: 79–128), and Randolph L. Braham. *The Politics of Genocide: The Holocaust in Hungary* (Detroit: Wayne State UP, 2000: 129, 145–146).

14 The story of the Oradea ghetto is documented in the diary of Éva Heyman and in the documentary novel, *Nine Suitcases,* of her stepfather, Béla Zsolt, both available in English, and by Canadian Teréz Mozes' memoir, *Staying Human Through the Holocaust* (Alberta: U of Calgary Press, 2005), as well as in several Hungarian-language memoirs. On Heyman and Zsolt see Louise O. Vasvári, "Hungarian Women's Life Writing in the Context of the Nation's Divided Social Memory, 1944-2014." *Hungarian Cultural Studies* 7 (2014): 55–81; http://ahea.pitt. edu/ojs/index.php/ahea/article/view/139. In Hungarian see Reuven Tsur (Steiner Róbert). *Menekülés a gettóból. Egy nagyváradi zsidó család története* (Flight from the Ghetto: The History of a Family from Nagyvárad) (Budapest: Norán, 2005) and Dániel Lőwy, "A sóa nagyváradi emlékíroi [The Memoirists of Nagyvárad]," *Várad* 8 (2010); http://www.varad.ro/node/267.

hood and having little contact with non-Jews other than servants, she did not personally experience antisemitic acts; antisemitism seemed distant to her. With the outbreak of war and the introduction of anti-Jewish laws, in spite of general fear and a sense of foreboding among her family, only her brother was determined to flee, though he was caught and deported with the rest of the family.

When the Jewish population was herded into the ghetto, the gendarmes were famously sadistic in their search for valuables, torturing many people in order to force them to divulge where they had hidden their valuables. Eva and her sister had received their first watches the previous year on their birthdays and, rather than be forced to hand them over, they smashed them and threw them into the fire. This event is seared in Eva's memory – in a time and place where children did not often receive gifts, the receipt of the first watch was an important symbol of the adolescent rite of passage.

Eva's description of the inhuman conditions of the trip by locked boxcar to Auschwitz and, on arrival, the subsequent humiliations for a religious young woman, is akin to the description offered by Zsuzsanna. The deportation train journey is such a traumatic, embodied, sensory and olfactory memory that it understandably appears in so many testimonial accounts of deportation and has become a collective genre of representation of "excremental assault" – the deliberate physical and mental torture and degradation and dehumanization of victims, who are deprived of space, sleep, food and especially of drink, and assaulted by odours of excrement, urine, vomit and dead bodies.[15]

Like Zsuzsanna and many other Hungarians, Eva was also not tattooed on arrival. She too describes the shaving of her head and how humiliating it was for her, a religious girl, to walk around naked in front of the Germans. Understandably, this is a scene that many more

---

15 On "excremental assault" see Terence Des Pres, *op cit.* 51–72.

female than male inmates describe in detail. The loss of hair was a more primal torment for them, cutting deeply into the self and causing the loss of their gender identity, mutilating it beyond recognition, so that even family members suddenly often did not recognize each other and felt like part of an indistinguishable mass. Eva and her sister, like Zsuzsanna and hers, were lucky enough to stay together, and were later sent from Auschwitz to Mittelsteine, a Nazi *Arbeitslager*, work camp, where the all female prisoners, primarily Jewish women from Hungary and Poland, laboured manufacturing component parts for the V-1 and V-2 rockets.[16] When the camp was liquidated, the Hungarian prisoners were transferred to Mährisch Weisswasser in the Sudetenland, where they were liberated by the Soviets. The Soviets did little to help the women, who feared them because they heard that Soviet soldiers were looking for women to rape.

~

The work that Hungarian women like Zsuzsanna and Eva performed as slave labourers is an important aspect of a vast and complex Nazi bureaucratic system of *Zwangsarbeit*, forced labour, that sustained the German economy and the economic needs of German industry of the Third Reich during World War II. The extent of German-operated *Arbeitslager* increased massively as the war progressed, with some fifteen million workers: about two-thirds from Eastern Europe, including forced labourers, civilians abducted from occupied countries, and slave labour by Jews from the camps. By the end of the war, virtually all surviving concentration camp inmates had spent at least

---

16 Two other memoirs that deal with life in the Mittelsteine camp are by Polish prisoners, Ruth Minsky Sender, *The Cage* (New York: Macmillan, 1986) and Sara Selver-Urbach, *Through the Window of My New Home: Recollections of the Lodz Ghetto* (Jerusalem: Yad Vashem, 1986, orig. Heb. 1964), part of which is a diary written in the camp itself between November 1944 and May 1945.

part of their captivity "leased out" by the SS to private companies, particularly to German defence industries, such as Thyssen, Krupp and IG Farben. It is estimated that about 20 per cent of Hungarian Jews sent to Auschwitz were used as forced labour, and of these, some 20,000 survived.[17] Paradoxically, Jewish women like Zsuzsanna and Eva likely survived the Holocaust because they were temporarily exempted from genocide due to the Third Reich's economic interests and labour shortages. At the same time, it is also true that surviving concentration camp inmates sent to Germany for slave labour were already marked for death through labour and would have perished had the war lasted a few months longer.

Zsuzsanna and Eva are both native-speaking Hungarian women of a similar age, social class, and religious and geographic background, both of whose experiences of the Holocaust include surviving Auschwitz and, subsequently, a labour camp in Germany and a final death march, in each case with a sister. As survivors who emigrated at different times after the war, both faced enormous linguistic and identity issues in writing about the traumatic memories and shattering experiences of their former lives.[18] A poignant feature of their testimonial writing, like that of many survivors, is that they write not merely to bear witness but also to memorialize those who perished. Their commitments to reconstructing their family history and remembering the dead in a kind of secular Kaddish serves at the same time to illustrate the history of a Central European Jewish culture erased by deportation, annihilation and displacement. By reframing history through their personal and family experiences and

---

17 Wolf Gruner, *Jewish Forced Labor under the Nazis: Economic Needs and Racial Arms, 1938–1944.* Tr. Kathleen M. Dell'Orto (New York: Cambridge UP, 2006).

18 Louise O. Vasvári. "Emigrée Central-European Jewish Women's Holocaust Writing." *Comparative Central European Holocaust Studies.* Eds. Steven Tötösy and Louise O. Vasvári (West Lafayette, IN: Purdue UP, 2009: 158–172).

by recounting everyday events left out of official history, they provide not merely source material for historians but also an alternative way of narrating the past, conveying the factual events and experiences of the Holocaust as well as their own individual sufferings and how they have coped with their memories.

In their testimonies, both Zsuzsanna and Eva recount some features of primarily female-gendered experiences of the Holocaust, such as familial bonding and the creation of surrogate families or "camp sisterhood," and the recounting, in such groups, of recipes and of stories from their former lives. These act as forms of spiritual resistance that safeguard their dignity and humanity and allow them to carry on the struggle to survive. [19]

It is not uncommon in testimonial writing that the narration devoted to the survivor's post-Holocaust life is the briefest and least detailed – stories of post-war immigration tend to serve more as a backdrop to the rebuilding of a life than to be concerned in depth with the new culture. Emphasis tends to be on recounting only the broad outlines of family life, professional success and involvement in local Jewish life. It is in this last "after" section that the two testimonies diverge significantly, with Zsuzsanna devoting few pages to post-Holocaust life and Eva providing a more detailed personal history. This difference of focus is likely due to the fact that Zsuzsanna was able to achieve a relatively stable life by 1949 and then, after the 1956 Hungarian Revolution, succeeded in emigrating to Toronto with her entire extended family of ten. Eva, on the other hand, suffered so many personal tragedies directly after liberation that, at one point, she describes an experience as "the most terrible, agonizing event in

---

19 Louise O. Vasvári. "Women's Holocaust Memories/Memoire: Trauma, Testimony and the Gendered Imagination." *Jewish Studies at CEU* 5 (2006–2007): 141–154.

[her] life ... worse even, than Auschwitz." While she was able to immigrate to Canada as early as 1948, she had to do so alone, and she faced many further struggles before marrying in 1959 and establishing a family.

Louise Vasvári
Stony Brook University/ New York University
2016

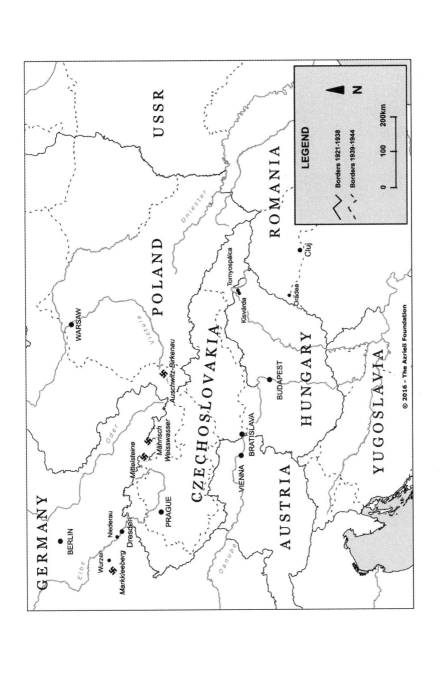

GERMANY

BERLIN

Wurzen

Niederau

Dresden

Markkleeberg

Mittelsteine

PRAGUE

Mährisch Weisswasser

Auschwitz-Birkenau

CZECHOSLOVAKIA

POLAND

WARSAW

USSR

Dniester

Oder

Vistula

Elbe

VIENNA

AUSTRIA

Danube

BRATISLAVA

BUDAPEST

HUNGARY

Kisvárda

Tornyospálca

ROMANIA

Oradea

Cluj

YUGOSLAVIA

LEGEND

Borders 1921-1938

Borders 1939-1944

0   100   200km

N

Zsuzsanna Fischer Spiro

Whoever reads my story, you must promise that you will remember and never forget. I tell my story to speak for the millions of innocent victims who cannot speak for themselves, to make sure that never again will this happen. I dedicate my story to my mother and to all the mothers who never lived long enough to know the joy of being a grandmother, and to my two wonderful sons, Peter and David, who represent the new generation of Jewish children born after the war, and who never knew the loving touch of a grandmother.

In memory of my mother, Gizella Funk Fischer.

A few years after liberation, realizing I would never be together with my mother again, I suddenly had an urge to visit her grave, even though I knew that she did not have one. Her ashes had been scattered over Poland or wherever the wind was blowing that day in June, 1944. My dear, beautiful mother, wherever you are, you never had a funeral or a gravestone. I loved you and will love you forever.

Foreword

When I saw the notice asking for people to help Holocaust survivors write their memoirs, I felt that it was my duty and obligation to work on this project. Being a child of two Holocaust survivors from Poland, it called to me personally. I think I was extremely lucky to be partnered with Zsuzsanna. When I first met her I was a little nervous and anxious, and I think she was a little hesitant. However, over the months I spent talking to her, we became friends and she opened up to me. After we had completed her memoir, I was touched when she told me that I knew her better than some of her friends of fifty years. Zsuzsanna told me that because of the Nazis and the war, her dreams of higher education and becoming a teacher had been destroyed. However, I think she *is* a teacher, telling her story and experiences of the war so that younger generations will know of the evil that the human race is capable of and how European Jewry suffered at the hands of not only the Nazis but also the bystanders, who were guilty of collaborating with the Germans or of simply doing nothing.

I found Zsuzsanna to be a very strong, intelligent woman. She had kept a diary of her experiences during the war and presented me with a translated manuscript that was invaluable in helping her finish her memoir. She described her experiences in great detail, giving me insight into what my mother must have experienced in the cattle cars and on her arrival in and departure from Auschwitz.

I have tremendous respect for Zsuzsanna and all that she has had to endure during her life – the loss of many of her family, her suffering during World War II, starting a new life after the war, escaping the Hungarian Revolution and having to once again start over and remake a life in Canada with her husband and children.

I have learned so much and will be forever grateful to the Azrieli Foundation and Zsuzsanna for this opportunity to work with her on her story.

Fran Weisman

My Peaceful Village

This is my living testimony.

I was born on November 18, 1925, in the small village of Tornyo-spálca, Hungary, but grew up in Kisvárda, a city that is almost three hundred kilometres from Budapest. My family and I moved there when I was twelve or thirteen. I had a loving mother, Gizella (née Funk) Fischer, who was born in August 1891 in Vásárosnamény, and father, Ervin Fischer, born January 22, 1890, in Kisvárda. My older brother, Endre (Bandi), was born November 5, 1920; my older sister, Klara (Klari), on July 1, 1922, and my younger brother, Tibor (Tibi), on January 23, 1929. Endre was born in Nagykároly, but the rest of us were born in Tornyospálca.

I had a typical, carefree childhood. Tornyospálca, where we first lived, was a small village. It was like any other small village – no paved roads, no transportation except carriages pulled by horses or cows, no electricity, no central heating, no telephone – and yet I still had a happy childhood. There was one main road in the town and our family lived on a side street. My father was the manager of a factory that made alcohol from potatoes. Our house had electricity, which was a big luxury then, and we had the first and only radio in the village. In the summer, my father would put it near the window and people came to listen to it. We also had chickens, geese, cows and a vegetable garden.

Life in the village was very peaceful. The majority of the villagers were not Jewish; there were about fifteen or twenty Jewish families in town. Mostly, we were friends with the other Jewish families. Everyone knew each other. The non-Jews worked on their farms and most of the Jewish people had a trade. There was one big store in the village that supplied groceries or materials – it was owned by a Jewish family – and there were two butcher stores owned by the Adler family. One was for kosher meat and the other one for non-kosher meat. They also owned a pub. We got together with them on Shabbat.[1] They had two daughters my age, Olga and Magda, with whom I was friends. Both of them perished in the war.

The Jewish children went to school with Christian children. I had non-Jewish friends but we weren't so close, and if I went to their houses, I couldn't eat anything because it wasn't kosher. There was a Catholic school and a Protestant school; one fall when the school year started, all the Jewish students from the Catholic school ended up being sent to the other school. We were never told why, but I believe that it was because the Catholic teacher was antisemitic. Every morning when it was time for prayers, the teacher told the Jewish students to go outside. We got along with the Christians and treated each other with respect. However, once I heard that the priest at Sunday church had told his congregation that the Jews were the ones who had killed Jesus. At the time, I didn't even know who Jesus was.

Now I am an eighty-eight-year-old woman living thousands of kilometres away from everything I left behind, having survived Hell. Still, I remember the happy little girl I was in Tornyospálca, who loved her family very much. Little did I know that my future loving and caring husband, Joseph Spiro, was living just a few kilometres

---

1 For information on Shabbat, as well as on other historical, religious and cultural terms; significant historical events and people; geographical locations; major organizations; and foreign-language words and expressions contained in the text, please see the glossary.

away in Gemzse. We married in 1949 and were married for sixty-two years, until his death, and I will love and miss him forever.

~

When I was twelve years old, my family moved to my father's birthplace of Kisvárda, where a lot of our relatives lived, because my father had gotten a job there. Kisvárda had a large Jewish population and a lot of Jewish cultural life to offer.

I went to high school for three years but unfortunately could not complete the fourth year of school. I loved school and, being a very good student, I had big plans for the future. However, all my plans and ambitions for my future came to an end because of the devil, Hitler. I will never forgive the Nazis and the Hungarians for this.

In 1940, I experienced my first disappointment. I was fifteen years old and in my third year of high school. The principal of the school was a fascist and an antisemite. He separated the Jewish girls from the gentile girls, using the excuse that there were too many students in the one room. Our new class was made up of Jewish girls and a few slow-learner gentile girls. However, we knew what the real reason was. I was very angry and hurt by this, and as a result I left school. The following year, my teacher asked me to return to school, but I was not willing to go back.

My mother told all her children to learn a trade because of the uncertainty of our future, so I learned to sew. At the time I was a teenager and didn't know very much about what was happening with the war; I don't know what my parents knew at the time, because they kept quiet about it. The first time I heard some news was around 1940 or 1941 when I met a Jew who had escaped from Poland to Hungary, hoping to have a better future in Hungary. He told me stories about what was happening in Poland and how the Jews were persecuted, but I never heard about the killings. Around this time, the Jewish men, including my father, who was already over fifty years old, and my older brother, Endre, were called into the Hungarian army. This was not the regular army but the Labour Service. The men did not wear army uniforms and they did not get guns. They were only "good" for the dirty work. After a few months, my father came back, but my brother was sent to the Russian front somewhere. He never returned and we will never know if he died from hunger, froze to death or was killed. He was only twenty-one years old when he disappeared.

The atmosphere was very antisemitic. We lived in constant fear, not knowing what would happen next. There were new Jewish laws that took everything away from us. Jewish people were not allowed to work. Signs were posted that said Jews and dogs were not allowed in the stores or other places. Jews were not allowed to own businesses. On the street, the Hungarians called us dirty Jews and we couldn't do anything about it, not because we were cowards but because there were only women and old men left. All the young men were in the army and even if they had been home, what could they have done with empty hands against loaded guns?

I remember a group of Hungarian men, who I think were mostly criminals released from jail, going from village to village stealing from the Jewish people. The huge Jewish community in Kisvárda often met up together at a marketplace, and one Sunday afternoon some Hungarians made speeches there. "Whose fault is it that the people are poor? The Jews! Whose fault is it that there is a war? The Jews!" If anything bad happened, it was always blamed on the Jews.

Bitter Tears

March 19, 1944, is a day that will live forever in my memory. This was the date that sealed our horrible future. On this day, the Germans invaded Budapest and took over the leadership in Hungary. There was a rumour that the Jews in the countryside would be safer than those in Budapest, but unfortunately this was not true, and most of the Jews who left Budapest, believing they would be safe, perished in Auschwitz. Our "dear" Hungarian-Christian friends left us to the mercy of the Germans. Those who were our friends became our enemies, and they turned away from us as if we had leprosy.

More laws against the Jews were introduced. One of the new laws was that all the Jews had to wear a yellow star. I remember the day we were ordered to wear the star as if it happened yesterday, and ever since then I have hated the colour yellow. I didn't go out of the house for days. I wasn't ashamed of being Jewish, but I felt so violated. The more they hurt us, the more proud I was to be Jewish, but I still only went out on the street when I really had to. I was only eighteen years old then, but I didn't want to see anybody. I was already fed up with everything. I didn't know that I should have been happy because I was still together with my family – my parents, my sister, Klari, and my brother Tibi. I didn't know that it would be only a few short weeks before things changed. How could anyone know that the devils from hell had been unleashed?

In early April 1944, during Passover, the Jewish population from the surrounding villages was taken to the ghetto in Kisvárda. They were allowed to take only a change of clothes and some food. At the end of April, we too had to leave our home and move into the ghetto, which was located in the most Jewish district of Kisvárda, by the synagogue and the surrounding area near Csillag and Petőfi Streets. All the Jewish people living within thirty to forty kilometres of Kisvárda were transported there and forced to live in the few streets of the ghetto.

Everybody knew which streets made up the ghetto. Hungarian gendarmes guarded the ghetto and the roadways were closed with barriers. Luckily, my family had some relatives who lived on a street that was part of the ghetto, so we stayed with them. We slept on the floor and had to share the room with strangers. Nobody had a separate room. I don't remember how we managed to eat because we were not given any food. We didn't have anything to do in the ghetto, so I helped mothers with their children and I also helped in the ghetto's kitchen. Most of the men were not there, as they had been sent to forced labour camps. Day after day, we became more frightened, but we were still hopeful that the situation would get better.

In late May 1944, all of the Jews were deported from the ghetto. The first time I saw a German officer was a few days before the deportations. When the German officers came, we were forced to stand in lines for hours until they counted us. They made a list with the name of every person; I never understood why, because within a few days many had already died, nameless, and those who were still alive and able to work were like walking skeletons. We became numbers on the lists the murderers kept.

The people from the ghetto were divided into two transports. The first one left on Monday, May 29, and the second transport left on Wednesday, May 31, 1944. There were rumours that we were being sent to Germany and that the young people would be working while the elderly would be watching the children. We didn't know anything about where we were going to be sent. We only knew who was going with the first transport and that our street was going to be sent on the second transport, so we were lucky that our family had two more days to be together. We cried as we said goodbye to our relatives and friends who were leaving on the first transport; although we didn't know what to expect, somehow we felt we would never see them again.

When the second transport left two days later, it was our turn to stand in line with our few bags. We didn't have anything else with us but I wished that the Germans had taken everything from us, even the clothes from our bodies, if only we had been allowed to stay together. I cannot express in words how terrible we felt. No one could imagine how horrific it was. To this day, when I think about the sickly elderly people who wanted only to die in peace where they had lived and the innocent babies who couldn't hurt anyone but would die because their great crime was to be born Jewish, I cannot hold back my tears.

Under the watchful eyes of the Germans, we walked to the train station. Our Hungarian "friends" were watching and laughing at us as we went by, waiting for the first chance to steal everything from our homes. It was very hot that day and we had to sit for hours at the train station. I almost fainted from thirst, and I am sure some people did. Finally, the train came – a cattle train. The soldiers counting us treated us like animals, forcing us into the cars of the train, sixty or seventy into each one. The only thing that was important was that my family stay together. Luckily, we were all in the same car. The doors were closed and locked from the outside. The conditions inside were awful. There wasn't any room to sit; there was no washroom, just a bucket in the corner; and we were not given anything to eat or drink. We were with strangers and we had to relieve ourselves in front of everybody. It was humiliating. It was so crowded we couldn't sleep. There were only two small windows in the wagon, and although they provided a little light so that we could tell if it was day or night, they didn't provide enough air.

The train stopped once, in a city called Kassa. I know this because someone saw the name of the station. Kassa, then a part of Hungary, is now called Košice and is in Slovakia. The doors were opened so that the bodies of those who had died between Kisvárda and Kassa could be removed; this gave the gendarmes a chance to take the remaining valuables from the Jews. People had hidden their jewellery; some had even hidden it in jars of jam. This was the last chance for the gendarmes to steal whatever they hadn't already taken from the Jews. Shortly after we stopped, the train started again, and over forty hours later we arrived in Hell. As I recall, we were on the train from May 31 until June 2.

It was dark when the train arrived in Auschwitz that Friday night, June 2, 1944. In my mind's eye, I saw the nice, familiar Friday nights when our mother used to light the Shabbat candles. This was the first time I turned against God, questioning, Why? When the cattle car's doors were opened we saw smoke, but at the time we didn't know what it meant. I saw SS guards and heard them playing a then-popular song called "Lili Marleen" on the accordion. I later asked myself the question that remains forever without an answer: How can they be happy and playing music when they know very well that in a few hours thousands of innocent people will be their victims? I was standing together with my family, not realizing that this would be the last time we would all be together. When I saw people in striped uniforms pushing the elderly, sick people in wheelchairs, I had no idea where they were being taken, but for some reason it gave me a slight hope of survival.

Then, in the dark night, we heard the terrible order that men had to be on one side and women had to be on the other. Everyone was crying and shouting. My brother and father went to one side, and we were calling their names to make sure that at least they were together. My sister, Klari, and I were on either side of our mother so that she was in the middle between us. The three of us were standing, holding each other's hands, when suddenly a flashlight was shone in our faces.

We were standing face to face with a man who, with his left or right hand, determined life or death, mostly death. He took my mother away from Klari and me, and for a few seconds it wasn't clear if I was to go with my mother or not, but then he asked me my age and decided to let me stay with Klari. My sister and I were told to go in one direction and my mother in the other. My mother took her scarf from her head and gave it to me, saying, "You have a cold, you need it more than I do." I had lost my scarf and had been sick on the train. When I didn't want to take it from her, she told me that her cousin had an extra one and she would get it from her. She went to another section with her relatives. I didn't know that soon they wouldn't need scarves anymore. I still don't remember if I had a chance to kiss her goodbye, and I didn't know that was the last time I would ever see her or feel her motherly love for me. This was the last we knew of our mother, who went with the other mothers and their darling little children to their deaths. It is so painful and hard to write about this.

We were standing in a separate line, tired, crying and waiting to see what our future would be. Our line was made up of women and girls from approximately eighteen to forty years of age. Some of the mothers were crying for their babies who had been taken away from them. Klari and I were crying for our mother and our loved ones. Then we started walking, not knowing where we were going.

There was a terrible smell in the air and we didn't have the slightest idea what it was. If we had known, I'm sure we would have all gone crazy. As we got closer to the camp, Birkenau, I started to scream because I saw human body parts burning in an open fire. One woman tried to calm me down and told me to stop screaming. She said I was imagining things, but I am sure she knew very well that I was right. Later, we found out that when the crematorium couldn't handle all the bodies, they were burned outside.

Slowly, dawn came, and I could see that everything was grey. There was no greenery, no grass, no birds. We had arrived at a building that was used as a bath house. First, we were told to strip naked and to leave our clothes in a certain place. We were told to keep our shoes and when Klari was told she could keep her glasses, we took it as a sign that we would stay alive.

The building was divided into different rooms and we had to wait in long lines. We didn't know what was happening to those who were ahead of us, but we didn't hear any screaming, so we figured that they were not being killed. Then it was our turn to go into the next room, where people shaved our hair until we were bald. They shaved not only our heads, but also all of our body hair, until we were totally hairless. Afterward, when I first saw those I knew, it was difficult to recognize one another. Then we were sprayed with some kind of chemical, had a shower, and were told to get dressed. We had to take whatever clothing there was. My first outfit was an evening gown and a pair of men's shorts for underwear. Some women were wearing men's clothes. I never saw my own clothes, my favorite outfit, again.

It was a bright, sunny day when I came out of this building, but I couldn't see anything except a wire fence. We had to stand in line again, five in every line, and we were guarded by the SS officers and German shepherd dogs as we arrived in the camp that was called C Lager, surrounded by electric wire fences. It was sure death if you touched the fence. The SS were watching us, and they were also standing guard in a watchtower. I don't understand why we had to be guarded so closely. After all, we were in rags, without hair, and there was an electric fence, but most of all we were sick at heart with no will or way to escape.

C Lager became our home. There were barracks in two rows. My barracks number was 15. The barracks had been built originally as stables for horses. There were no beds and we had to sit on the muddy dirt floor with our feet spread out so the person in front of us could sit between our legs. We sat like this, with five in every line.

I do not remember clearly what happened in those first few days in the barracks; I can only thank God and my sister, Klari, that I survived. According to my sister, I didn't respond to anything, even when they gave orders to stand in line or to do this or that. I did not care about anything. I almost lost my mind. I only remember being very cold and asking for a blanket to keep warm, the kind we used to have in our home, and when Klari said that we didn't have it anymore I was so confused that I asked her to give me my father's winter coat.

Every dawn, we had to stay in line, five in every row, and it was the same every evening. From then on we were always in rows of five, even when we were given something to eat. I don't know what they gave us to eat, but it wasn't like any food I had ever had before. I can't even try to explain how horrible it tasted. The first person in line was given a bowl, which she passed back to the next person behind her until it reached the end of the line, and if there was something left then it went again, from mouth to mouth. This was how we ate our food with strangers. We didn't even have a spoon.

Meanwhile, without any warning or reason, the Nazis continued with the selections to send people to the gas chamber. From the barracks, we had to go through a door in single file, and if they didn't like the way a person looked, or for no reason at all, they just grabbed her and sent her to the other side, which meant certain death. Those people selected were never seen again. I saw unfortunate sisters, crying, separated from each other, each one left alone.

One day, Klari came to me with great happiness to say that she had met our cousin Anna from Vásárosnamény. We were both so naïve – this made us hopeful that maybe our mothers, who were sisters, were alive and together. Anna was there with her three sisters. Anna was the oldest, and she wanted us to be together with them. Their barracks had wooden bunk beds and they had grey blankets that had been used for the horses, but for us it was a luxury compared to sitting on the dirt floor in our barracks.

At that time, I developed a problem with eating. I could not swallow even the small portion of food that we were given. I could eat only the small bit of bread, which I don't think was really bread, and some margarine. Later I was very ashamed when I found out that

Anna had given me her portion of bread just to keep me alive, God bless her memory. When she could no longer tolerate that I wasn't eating, she slapped my face. I cried, not because I was mad at her but because I was grateful. I knew that she wanted to keep me alive and she had done it for my own good.

Each day, the number of prisoners grew smaller and smaller, and more and more bodies were delivered to the entrance of the Lager in grey horse blankets. We were not put to work, and we lived in constant fear. As the selections continued, we wondered how long we would stay together. Finally, one day we all had to gather in the middle of the Lager. There were thirty-two barracks in the Lager with more than four hundred people in each barracks and, within a few moments, there were thousands and thousands of us standing in line. We all had to undress and stand naked; we were so emaciated that we looked like skeletons.

The selection took place near the kitchen, which was near the entrance of the Lager. Again we saw our friends crying, sisters who were already marked for death standing in a special circle. Then it was Klari's and my turn. We had to stand with our left arms held up high in the air. I don't know why we were told to raise our left arms. We were told to turn around, and then the officer doing the selection sent us to separate sides. In my panic, I didn't remember which one of us was supposed to go to the left, which we knew meant that we had only a few more hours of suffering left. Suddenly, a miracle happened. Klari called out, in Hungarian, "lánytestvér," sister, and I said, in German, "my sister." A Hungarian doctor standing nearby told us that no one was supposed to know that we were sisters. But the officer then told us both to turn around again, and he sent Klari and me to the right. This was the second time that, by a miracle, I survived. Right in front of him, Klari and I started kissing each other, which was a mistake because their goal was to make us unhappy and suffer. I am not a strong believer in miracles, especially after what happened to our people, but there it was, a miracle. I felt that my mother was watching over us. I don't know if that happened to anybody else. After the selection, Anna and her sisters were sent to another Lager, and I was sad to see them go, but at least they were together. I later wrote in my diary that I would "never be able to forget that Anna took care of us with such selfless love. I could write pages and pages about it."

Later we found out that Anna and her sisters had been sent to the neighbouring B Lager, which I heard was a work Lager. There was only the electric wire fence between us. Sometimes, from a distance, we were able to see each other through the fence. After that selection, we went back to our barracks. It was almost empty, and everyone was crying for their loved ones who were no longer here. I could smell the terrible odour as the bodies of the victims were burned. The chimneys were working day and night, and there were more and more selections almost daily. Again, I would have to say it was a miracle that Klari and I were still together. Somebody was watching over us.

One day, after another selection, we were taken from C Lager to B Lager, the same one where our cousins Anna, Bozsi, Klari and Iren were. It was a very strict Lager, and so it was impossible to be with them in the same barracks, but at least we had a chance to see each other from time to time. In early June 1944, when we had first arrived in C Lager, we could see through the fence to B Lager, where there had been entire families together, with children and the elderly. We heard they were from Czechoslovakia. One morning in July 1944, we woke up and it was very quiet. Not a sound was heard from the other side, and we saw that the Lager was empty. We suspected that they had been sent to their deaths during the night, making room for us. When we came to B Lager we were very upset to find the personal belongings and family pictures they had left behind, and we had the sad job of burning these. I especially remember the pictures of a young boy and girl, tied together with a pink ribbon. With a broken heart, I wondered what had happened to those two young people. Where were they now? I never knew them, but I cried for them. I imagined their young faces disappearing in the flames. I also see the little children's shoes. Who wore them? I am tortured by these memories that are still with me, yet I don't want to forget. I feel it is my duty to recall them and to write about them. Having survived, I owe this to them. I also feel it was my duty to bring more Jewish children into the world to keep our heritage alive.

Who I Used To Be

Life in B Lager was always the same. There was roll call early every morning and another at night, as we stood with five in every line. Under the SS men and women, the *Blockälteste* were in charge of us. The *Blockälteste* were the prisoners who had been assigned as block leaders in the camp. I am ashamed to admit that these Jewish girls were not much better to us than the Germans were. When I first arrived in Auschwitz-Birkenau, one of them welcomed us with the greeting, "You came through the door and you will leave through the chimney." At the time, I didn't have the slightest idea what she was talking about.

I suspected that the Germans put something in our food, because I do not think that I was rational. I also believe that is why I and many other women didn't get our periods anymore, though others have said that this was due to malnutrition. In this new Lager, we lost our identities completely. We were tattooed with numbers on our arms. I was no longer Zsuzsanna Fischer but A12396. I still do not understand why I was so afraid of having the number. I cannot describe what it was like to become a nameless slave; I was no longer a human being, only a number. When I look at my number today, I realize that this number is the shame of the Germans and not my shame.

Although B Lager was a work camp, we didn't do any work there. This was the Lager from which labourers were sent all over Germany to replace those who had died or were unable to work anymore and had been killed. In one of the next selections, Klari and I were chosen to be sent out for work. We were happy to leave Auschwitz, the smell and the smoke. However, when we were examined again before leaving, red spots were found on my stomach. Since the Germans thought it was an infection, I was kept back, but luckily Klari was kept back with me. I don't think the red spots were anything, probably a result of the diet – we weren't given a piece of fruit or a vegetable for the entire summer. Later I found out that the transport I missed had been sent to a Lager that was next to the one where my father and brother were. However, the important thing was that Klari and I were still together, because I am sure that without each other, neither one of us would have survived.

In late September 1944, although I don't know how we knew the date, we celebrated Yom Kippur, shivering in the same rags that we had been given in the summer. I recall being taken to a city where a group of us were sprayed with some chemical to disinfect us. This was the first time we had left the Lager since June and, naturally, we were accompanied by SS men and their German shepherd dogs. At first, I was anxious to leave the Lager, but I was very disappointed when I did. While we were in the Lager, I wasn't really thinking about life outside the fence, but then I saw that outside of the camps, life was going on as if everything was normal. It made me sick to see German mothers with their children and flowers in their gardens, so when we had to go back to the Lager I didn't mind being surrounded by the wire fences, because I didn't want to see how life was for everyone else on the outside.

Finally, in early October 1944, we left Auschwitz. Klari and I were sad to say goodbye to our cousins, but we took comfort in the fact that they were still together and that Klari and I were together. As I mentioned, one of our cousins was also named Klari. We didn't know then that we would never see her again – she died on her way home when she was eighteen years old.

After leaving the Lager, we stood in line for hours, waiting for our orders without knowing where we were going to be sent. Would we be sent to work or to die? We hoped it would be far away from the crematorium, which was still running day and night.

After walking for miles, we came to a building that reminded us of the one we had first seen on our arrival in Auschwitz. This building was also divided into separate sections, and we had to walk single file down a very dark, narrow hall. We didn't know what was happening to those who were ahead of us in line, but the SS were standing behind hidden doors. We only saw them at the last moment. We had to walk by them as they played their favourite game, which was to take certain girls from the line, and of course these girls were never seen again. Klari and I made it through to the outside, thankful that we were still alive. Then, we got onto a cattle train. We must have still been valuable to the Germans, because in every wagon two SS officers were guarding us, even though I am sure it would have been impossible to escape.

Shortly after the train left it had to stop because of a terrible air raid. It seemed as if there were bombs for everywhere except for Auschwitz. I know that with two or three bombs the Allies could have saved millions and millions of lives, since the Germans would not have been able to rebuild Auschwitz and continue with their mass murders. This will forever remain a shame for the entire world, as after the war it was discovered that the Allies knew about the trains and the gas chambers; I suspect they closed their eyes because it was happening to the Jews.

After a few days of travelling, the train arrived at a small town called Markkleeberg, which was part of Leipzig, Germany. Compared to Auschwitz, it was almost like a nice resort town. The biggest difference was that there was no chimney, no smoke and no terrible smell from the burning of Jewish martyrs. This was a small Lager with a few barracks. Relative to Auschwitz, the barracks seemed luxurious – each one had a washroom. In Auschwitz, the bathroom was a large room the size of a barracks, which could hold about a thousand people. The toilets were just holes cut into large boards that we sat on. It was so humiliating. While we were sitting and relieving ourselves, male Jewish prisoners from another Lager came to clear out our feces from underneath us. In Auschwitz, we could not shower for almost five months, but in Markkleeberg we could, though only with cold water. When I started writing a diary about my time here, this is what I began with: *A whole new chapter starts in my little book. I will remember the days spent here as the highlight of our Lager life. It was here that we started to live almost like human beings again.*

In the barracks, there was a single bed with a blanket for every person. There was no heating, and when it became very cold Klari and I slept together so that we had double blankets to keep us warm. In every other way, this Lager was a miniature Auschwitz, with SS men and women, the deadly wire fence and the dogs; and every morning and evening we had to stand in line to be counted.

Over the first few days, we had to do very difficult work, carrying stones. I don't remember where we carried them or why, but they were very heavy. The Sunday after we arrived was the first time we were given some meat and potatoes to eat, foods we hadn't had in the previous five months. There wasn't very much food but it was enough to keep us alive. More and more transports arrived in the Lager and with the growing numbers the food situation became worse and worse.

I had been there about two weeks when we all received grey uniforms and from then on we were working for our German enemies in a Junkers airplane factory. Our work helped their war effort, but we had no choice – it would have been certain death to refuse. I worked on a very specialized machine; there were only two in the whole factory. We worked twelve hours during the day one week and twelve hours during the night the following week. If we did a good job we were given some coupons with which we could buy something at a little store there. I bought myself a pair of wooden shoes as a present.

I still do not understand how we were able to work twelve hours a day under those conditions. Then again, I can't understand a lot of other things that happened as well.

When we weren't working, our roommates' favourite topic was exchanging recipes. It made me sick just to listen to it, but maybe they thought that speaking of food would help them to forget how hungry they were. Every evening, we got our daily bread and margarine portion. I don't remember what we had to eat during the day. The bread we got in the evening was also for the next day. Some girls ate their whole bread right away, wanting to at least feel they had something in their stomachs, but Klari and I did not eat it all at once. Klari had a special talent for slicing the bread with a wooden knife in order to save half of it. She was able to cut the thinnest slice of bread, and thanks to her I always had a whole slice saved for the next day. This meagre portion of bread was priceless. We were always hungry and every morning before we left for the factory we hid our bread under our uniforms to prevent anyone from stealing it from us. We had to be very careful to keep it hidden, because if the guards had seen the bread they would have taken it away.

One evening, I turned against Klari. I knew she was only saving the other half of the bread for our own good, but I told her that I was going to go along with the rest of the girls and eat my entire portion of bread. One never knew what would happen tomorrow. She argued with me but gave me my share; however, I changed my mind and decided to save some for the next day. When it was breakfast time, I looked through the machines to see if she was eating her bread and I ate my bread at the same time as her. So, my independence lasted for less than a day and that evening we cried together, saying, "What would our mother say if she knew we'd had an argument over a piece of bread?" You cannot imagine what hunger can drive a person to do.

The rest of the weeks and months went by without any changes. One day, my machine didn't work and we called the foreman. He tried to fix it, without success. I was standing there next to him, shaking, because everybody was afraid of him. After a while, still not able to fix the machine, he asked me, "Do you know what this is? It's sabotage." Then he started singing and spoke to me again, saying, "Do you know what the penalty for sabotage is? Death." I was terrified.

One day, there was an air raid and somebody said that the foreman had been killed, but to our disappointment he was back a short time later. There were more and more air raids and somehow we knew that the Allies couldn't be very far away. Unfortunately, this worked against us. When we were working at night, instead of being able to sleep during the day we had to go to a bomb shelter, which wouldn't have saved us anyway. How many times we wished that the guards would just let us sleep instead of making us go to the shelter.

In my diary, I wrote down a song that someone had written in the camp.

> *I am no longer who I used to be.*
> *I am a prisoner in Markkleeberg, a small number in*
> *a big prison camp.*
> *All I have left is hope.*
> *With aching heart, with tired body, I've been made to*
> *work night after night.*
> *I am weeping bitter tears. I feel I cannot bear it*
> *anymore.*
> *I am no longer who I used to be.*
> *I don't have a real home, in a foreign land, left all*
> *alone.*
> *A heavy sorrow weighs on my soul.*
> *In my dreams I always return home.*
> *If only I could go home once again, I would come to*
> *you softly, quietly.*
> *I would embrace you without a word, and I would*
> *cry bitterly.*
> *Oh, dear, I would cry so bitterly.*

Our Strength

At the beginning of April, we noticed that the Germans were act-
ing strangely. Soon after, on Friday, April 13, 1945, we didn't have to
go to work. We could hear the noise from the battleground, and we
just knew that the war couldn't last much longer. Then the Germans
ordered us to leave the Lager immediately. We didn't know what to
do. Some of us were thinking about hiding in the Lager, believing
that the American army would be arriving shortly, but if the Germans
were to find us they would have killed us immediately. Some of the
women did hide, but having lived through almost a year of suffering,
Klari and I decided not to hide and to go with the transport because
we didn't want to die in the last days of the war. Klari and I took the
valuable piece of bread we had saved and left the Lager that night
with the other prisoners, toward the uncertain future. The Germans
knew they had lost the war and didn't have too much time left, and
still they would not leave us in the Lager to await the Americans. We
Hungarian Jews were their last victims.

Later, we heard that we would be liberated the next day. I was so
hoping this was true, and that a few hundred lives would be saved
and our suffering would soon end. As we were walking, the Germans
guarded us, promising that we were going to a different Lager. I know
it sounds strange, but even after all these years I clearly remember
how much I wished to be in a Lager and not outside walking. At least

the Lager would have protected us from the cold wind and rain and we would have had a roof over our heads. The Germans didn't say anything except "Schnell!" (Fast!) I am sure that they didn't have any idea where they were taking us and were just exerting their power over us until the last minute. I wrote in my diary:

We began our wanderings just like our ancestors did thousands of years ago. We started out at night and marched all day Saturday. That's when I realized how strong a person can be. We spent the first night in a town called Wurzen under God's open sky. Perhaps that was the biggest disappointment of my life because our guards had kept promising us all along that we'd end up in a Lager. I cannot express in words what new meaning the word Lager took on, this nasty word that has become associated with more and more painful memories. What wouldn't we have given just to lay our completely exhausted heads on a bare bed of planks, after a long, arduous, back-breaking trip. The only ones who can understand this are people like us who live the bleak, joyless life of the homeless. In other words, the sad reality dawned on us that we would be sleeping outdoors. At daybreak: "Immer weiter" [Keep pushing on]. Oh, my God, how much suffering these two words can encompass.

We were near a small forest when suddenly we saw planes flying above us. They flew very low, and I am sure that they saw that we were not soldiers because they didn't shoot at us. But we were still frightened. We didn't sleep through the night. The next day, the soldiers let us lie down in an open yard, but it was impossible to sleep. The only clothing we wore was the uniforms from the factory. I couldn't even close my eyes for a moment, partly because I was so cold and hungry but mostly because there was a bright light shining down on us from the sky. I don't know what it was, but the Soviets were using it. At this point, we were closer to the Soviets than the Americans. Sometimes I still have nightmares about this bright light.

Sunday, Monday, Tuesday, Wednesday, Thursday were uneventful days, I must say, even though every minute, every hour, brought new horrors. In the meantime: airplanes droning overhead, machine guns ra-ta-tat-tatting; and after each occurrence it's becoming more apparent that the good Lord has different plans for us, perhaps that we should live happily with our loved ones again. On Thursday afternoon, after one of these attacks, we stopped for a rest in a village called Niederau. On Friday morning, after having spent an extremely cold night, we woke up in the middle of a very flat area, not a tree in sight to shelter us from the strong winds of the uplands. In the meantime, the air temperature kept dropping, and we could tell by the clothing of the people and the vegetation around us that we had reached higher and higher altitudes. In the morning when we woke up, there were fires going in several places, and some of the craftier women had already started cooking. Some were making nettle soup, others potatoes, depending on what provisions they had. Meanwhile, our guards kept encouraging us, saying that we would get something to eat. We also managed to cook a plateful of potatoes; our bread supply hadn't run out yet thanks to Klari's careful rationing, which I had so often objected to.

Our shoes fell apart from all the walking, so we threw them away; and still we were able to go on, but not everybody could. Our numbers became fewer and fewer. The Germans didn't bother to count us anymore. When we saw the bodies lying on the road, we could do no more than look at them and walk by. Whoever was able to, still had to walk – *schnell*. Even after all these years, I wonder how I survived.

With broken hearts we walked through cities, usually in the dark. I looked through the windows where people were sleeping, families peacefully together, while we were like criminals in the dark. There was no place to stop to rest our tired bodies. Besides, it was better to be in the forest or just about anywhere else, as long as we were not among people reminding us that we had once had our own families and homes. It was especially difficult to be among the German civilians. We didn't look like human beings anymore.

After a week, we received our first two slices of bread and eight to ten potatoes per person, depending on how the goddess Fortuna bestowed her favours. Everyone calmed down, and we set off between 5:00 and 6:00 p.m. with our stomachs growling less. All night long, we marched on in the vicinity of Dresden, coming within two kilometres of the city. Toward dawn we caught sight of the long-awaited forest, which would serve as the place where we could rest for the coming day and night. Given that it was a Saturday morning, we didn't want to start cooking, and so we took a rest on the wet grass. Our bed linen consisted of two coats without any lining. We lay down on one and used the other as a covering; you can just imagine how much warmth they provided. We must have slept from 7:00 to 11:00, when the rain forced us to sit up. We moved further into the forest, taking our belongings with us. These consisted of two pillowcases that we carried slung over our shoulders and a handbag made of the same material, treasures that came from the Lager.

It was pouring, and our predicament was becoming more and more unbearable. I was sitting under a tree, snuggling up to Klari, and the images of the past went through our minds, leaving painful marks: unforgettable Saturday afternoons that could be so intimate and beautiful. "Austreten!" [Leave, get moving!] was soon heard, and in the middle of a wild downpour, we started clambering upward for about fifty metres. The ground under our feet was sodden. If we managed to take a step upward, we slid back two. I don't even know what it was, perhaps some supernatural power that helped us get up there. Klari moved more easily than me, and so with her help I felt solid ground under my feet after a while.

April 20 is a date that will forever be painful; our company was assembled and the sad procession started off. Our journey led us past family houses, homes; from behind flowered curtains, happy mothers with their children would look at us either with pity or with scorn and malicious glee. And I, who couldn't hurt a fly, was filled with a desire for revenge, and in tears implored the good Lord to help us and make them experience what we were now going through.

We kept moving, obliviously, we were hanging on to each other, and soon we realized that we either were ahead of the group or had fallen behind, or perhaps the darkness was impenetrable, but there was not a soul around us. We quickened our pace, and then we spotted two unsteady figures up ahead: they were Ella and Dita Schatten. We joined them and together recited the traditional Saturday evening prayer, then dragged ourselves further along. We remembered again those Saturday evenings when we used to say the prayers with our dear, sweet mother.

In deep silence, immersed in our own thoughts, we were alerted by the voice of the Blockälteste, "Kids, line up in rows of five, the word is that we're going to have a roof over our heads." We obeyed almost mechanically, but less than 25 per cent of our group would dare to hope that it was even a possibility we'd have a stable or a loft. We collapsed onto our bundles, some falling asleep, others entertaining thoughts of escape. It stopped raining, but the cold was almost unbearable. Around 10:00 or 11:00 we received the happy news and set out. Part of the group ended up in a stable, and we were taken to another village; that's how we lost Ella. A loft covered with hay, our fondest wish; by the eighth night we had a roof over our heads again.

⌒

About three or four days later, when we were resting for a few hours in a forest, we began to wonder how long we could go on like this – should we try to escape? It couldn't last much longer. Was it worth taking a risk? But when it was time to leave, we left the forest and joined the transport. Shortly after, we heard shots and realized that some unfortunate girls who had decided to stay would now stay there forever.

It seemed to us as if we had been walking in circles. On one side there were the Soviets, and on the other side there was the US army, and still the soldiers didn't let us go. However, we noticed some changes in their behaviour. The SS guards were not watching us as closely as before. Maybe they finally realized that their days were numbered. One night, Klari and I decided to escape from the group and hide in a small building in a lumberyard with two other girls who were also sisters. Suddenly I felt like a bird escaping from a cage. Having been slaves for so long, we didn't know what to do with our sudden freedom. The only thing we did know was that we couldn't stay there.

We were constantly hungry, but sometimes we found some raw potatoes a farmer had forgotten in the ground. Our only concern was to survive. How could we avoid our enemies in a strange land? We were still wearing our rags and looked like skeletons. The Germans could tell just by looking at us who we were and where we had come from. Our plan was to go in the opposite direction just like the Germans were doing. They were escaping from their homes and from their enemies.

We realized that if we wanted to survive, we would have to do something to help ourselves. We started begging, but most of the time we stole, because we needed food and clothing. I am not ashamed to admit that I had become an expert in stealing; this was the only way to survive. We couldn't depend on anyone for help. Besides, the Germans had stolen everything from us, especially our loved ones, and this could never be repaid.

We never stayed longer than one day in the same village, because we were afraid of being captured. It was still Germany, still enemy territory. Then, one day our freedom came to a sad end. Klari and one of the sisters we had met earlier were waiting for me and the other sister at a meeting place we had decided on earlier. After we had finished our usual begging or stealing trip, we returned to the meeting place to find that they were not there. We didn't know where to go or what to do except cry. We still knew how to cry. We were still human beings

even if we didn't look like it. Finally, after what seemed like an eterni-
ty, we saw some people walking toward us, and when they got closer,
to my indescribable happiness, I recognized Klari and the other sister.
Klari told me later that they had been caught but had begged the SS to
let them look for us. This was another miracle.

Our short period of freedom was over, and once again we were
slaves, just a few days before the war ended. I don't know why, but instead of shooting us, the SS walked with us to the next village to meet
up with another transport. The prisoners in this transport had been
captured from different places and were a mixture of different nationalities, mostly Polish women, not all of whom were Jewish. They were
not very friendly, but perhaps they had suffered more than us, if that
was even possible.

We were in the forest when somebody came with wonderful news
that the German soldiers were changing from their uniforms into civilian clothes and were leaving. I was so weak I couldn't stand up; I
will never forgive myself for not having crawled on my knees to see
the big cowards escape. Without their guns and whips in their hands
they were nobodies, trying to save their worthless lives.

After a short rest, we left the forest with no idea where to go in
this strange country that we had every reason to hate. There we were,
barefoot and with short hair, and everywhere we went people knew
who we were by the way we looked. Nobody cared about us. It was
as if we were still slaves. We were hungry and couldn't remember the
last time we had eaten anything, so we went knocking on doors begging for some food. We found an old woman who was feeding her cat,
and she divided the food between her cat and us. How I hated that
cat. I was angry at the poor cat, because I was sure that she had had
breakfast that day while we had not.

We had been liberated by the Soviets on Tuesday, May 8, 1945, the
day Germany surrendered. I saw German officers on the street stripping their ranks from their uniforms in the hope that they would
look like plain soldiers and not SS, making it easier to escape their

well-deserved punishment. I hope they didn't. I had never hated any-body in my life before, but the Nazis taught me to hate, and even now, after so many years, I still feel the same way about them. Unfor-tunately, I will never be able to escape from my nightmares and my painful memories.

At that time, we never knew where we would be sleeping the next night or what we would have to eat. Naturally, Klari and I wanted to go home because we were hoping that we would find some of our family waiting for us. We were not far from Czechoslovakia, but there wasn't any means of transportation. Sometimes we were able to get a short ride on a truck, but mostly we walked to get home, as if we hadn't walked enough from April 13 to May 8 under the Germans. Sometimes we stood for hours at a train station, hoping to get on a train that would take us closer to home, a home that we didn't realize no longer existed.

Finally, we arrived in Bratislava, and for the most part we found the people there friendly, which was very different from our previous experience. The American Jewish Joint Distribution Committee, or the Joint, an organization supported by Jews from the US, had been established there and found us a place to stay with a gentile woman who said that her husband was Jewish but that he hadn't survived. She was very nice to us and gave us a bed to sleep in. We even went to a restaurant to eat. Even though our situation had improved, Klari and I were restless to go home to find out if any of our loved ones had survived and might be waiting for us there. When we walked by the shore of the Danube River, I thought of Hungary on the other side. Standing there by the shore, I am ashamed to admit that I was home-sick for the country that had treated me so badly.

Together

I had my first feeling of happiness in Bratislava when Klari and I coincidentally met a man on the street who was from Kisvárda. We recognized each other and he told us that he had seen our father about two weeks earlier! This was the first news we had heard about our family in almost a year. After this, Klari and I began to hope again and tried even harder to find some kind of transportation to get home. We finally arrived in Budapest on June 10, 1945. Remembering our aunt Margit's address in Budapest, we were able to find her. To our great joy, our grandmother was also there! She could not believe her eyes when she saw us; she cried for so long that I thought she was never going to stop. We were the first ones from the whole family to return. After the news about the treatment of the Jews had reached Budapest, she and my aunt were afraid that nobody from the family had survived.

My grandmother and aunt had spent some terrible months in the ghetto in Budapest but, thankfully, had survived. Fortunately, there hadn't been enough time for the Germans to liquidate the ghetto. I was told that the young people from Budapest had been sent to work in Germany. Most of them hadn't survived. They also told me about the Nyilas, or Arrow Cross, a fascist, antisemitic party that had assumed power in Hungary in October 1944 and assisted the SS in the deportation and killing of the Jews. The Nyilas murdered thousands of Jews by shooting them into the Danube River.

A few days after we found our grandmother and aunt, our uncle Miklos returned. He was Margit's husband and my father's younger brother. Unfortunately, their two wonderful sons, Pista and Feri, our first cousins, never came back. They had been in their early twenties, may their poor souls rest in peace.

Just as in Bratislava, there was a Joint organization in Bethlen Square in Budapest to help those who had returned from the war. Klari and I had registered our names, as had other survivors, and we went there every day to check the list of names of those who had survived the camps. One day, to our great joy, we found our father's name on the list! Klari and I ran back to tell our grandmother the good news. Although she was in her late seventies, she walked all the way there, not because she didn't believe us but because she wanted to see with her own eyes the name of her son on the list of survivors.

About a week later, I was sitting in the back of the apartment when I heard my grandmother screaming from the kitchen. Fearing something had happened to her, I ran to her – and suddenly saw my father coming up the stairs. It was an emotional reunion, especially when he told us that our brother Tibi had survived with him. Until that moment I'd had no knowledge of Tibi's fate, because his name had not been on the list of survivors. Klari and I ran to Bethlen Square to find him. He had not heard any news about us, either, and when we saw each other there the three of us kissed and hugged endlessly.

Now the four of us – Klari, Tibi, my father and I – were together. I thought I was dreaming. Unfortunately, my mother and brother Endre never came back. This is how we started our sad lives together; instead of six it was just the four of us, and it was never the same as before the war, without my mother and eldest brother. After a few days of rest, we knew we had to start our new life without them. Klari and I had visited Kisvárda and Vásárosnamény for a few days before our father and Tibi had come back because we had cousins there. We had travelled there on the top of railway cars. When we had been in Kisvárda we were unable to find anything from our home before the war, not even a piece of furniture, so we knew we had to start all over again, except we didn't have any idea how.

Eventually my father decided that he would go back with Tibi to Kisvárda to look around, and Klari and I would stay in Budapest until they could make some living arrangements for all of us. At the time, finding transportation was still difficult. Somehow my father found a truck driver who was willing to take him and my brother to Kisvárda. As soon as they left, Klari and I decided to run after them and go with them. We felt that we had been separated long enough and now that we had found each other, we wanted to stay together.

I don't know how long it took for me to realize that I had to start a new life if I wanted to survive. I have a good memory, but somehow those first few days and weeks are not clear. It took some time before I understood that I had my freedom back, but I didn't know how to use it, what to do or how to start living again. I could wake up when I felt like it and eat when I was hungry if we had food.

My family and I moved back into our old home, since it was completely empty. Some of our non-Jewish neighbours said that more Jews were coming back than had left, and they were absolutely not delighted to see us. I had a bad feeling about them, even though some of them were nice to us. I just couldn't forgive them for what had happened to us.

My father was fifty-five years old when the war ended. I heard that of the entire Jewish population of Kisvárda, only three men who were older than fifty had come back and that not one woman over forty had returned. All of us in the family were broken both in spirit and physically, but somehow we managed to lead a fairly normal life. Soon we heard that some people were marrying and a new generation of Jewish children was being born. My father got work as the manager of an alcohol factory, and eventually I was able to get a job sewing for a Jewish friend of mine. Sadly, my mother wasn't there to tell me that I was just twenty years old and could go back to school to follow the dream I had had before the war.

Most of the Jewish people who had survived realized that there was no future in Hungary for the Jews and moved away from our city to Israel, to the United States or to Canada. Many who left were single, but we were a family, together, and we decided to stay in Kisvárda.

Into the Foreign Winter

When I met my husband, Joseph (Józsi) Spiro, another Hungarian Holocaust survivor, I wasn't thinking about marriage. In June 1949, I went to visit my aunt in Budapest and he and I met each other there. We started to go out and became engaged at the end of July. I stayed with my aunt Margit until our wedding on September 11, 1949, in Budapest in the Dohány Synagogue. Joseph had his own apartment, and so I had a home again, where I belonged, and a good husband. Who could ask for anything more?

Unfortunately, since I met and married my husband after the war, I never had a chance to meet his family. His mother, Pepi Klein Spiro, his brothers Bela and Dezso, and his sisters Margit, Hermina and Regina, all perished during the war. Only his sister Ilona (Ilus), who had been in Budapest, survived.

When I became pregnant, we were excited to start our family but there was more suffering to come. Our son George (Gyurika), who was named after my husband's late father, was born on June 11, 1950. We were so delighted, but the doctor gave us the bad news that he was sick. Sadly, we lost him when he was eleven months old. We buried him in Budapest. My sister, my five cousins and a few other women all had first-born babies who died as well.

On February 25, 1952, our son Peter was born in Budapest, and on April 7, 1955, our son Gabor (David) was born there as well. Just over one year later, in October 1956, I began writing in my diary again when a new trauma befell us.

October 22, 1956

For us, the series of events started on this day, because even though it was a day like any other, at night we were awakened by a loud knocking. Our Tibi arrived, accompanied by two detectives. He'd been arrested on a false charge, and they'd come for the money that was supposedly at our place. We felt awful, but unfortunately there was nothing we could do. On October 23, Klari and I went to Erzsébet, where he was imprisoned. Later Józsi came too, but unfortunately we came away despondent, without having seen Tibi for even a second. At home we heard talk about a student demonstration, but we didn't pay it much heed. Granted, it was unusual, but we were preoccupied with our own problem. Klari and I decided we'd go that evening to visit the woman who worked for Tibi. We were hoping to learn something about the circumstances of his arrest from her. Although people warned us that there were huge crowds on the streets and the trams were not running, we didn't let it hold us back.

Indeed, unusual anti-Russian slogans filled the air, and the workers were whizzing by on trucks, shouting anti-communist messages. I went to the place we'd agreed on, but Klari and I left disappointed because we didn't find out anything. We went to see a lawyer, entrusting the case to him, and we came away at ten o'clock feeling reassured, knowing that he would go to the police station the next day. After a long wait, we got on a tram that had to stop at Wesselényi Street because of the trams blocking its way. By then traffic had come to a total standstill. The crowd surged along the street. Although we were worried about getting home, we mingled with the crowd and were carried along with the flow. At Dohány Street, we heard an unfamiliar sound, and in an instant everyone came to a shocked halt. News of shooting and fighting at the radio station spread fast, and the strange sound we heard was gunfire. It gave us a terrible feeling, but we kept on walking. At Rákóczi Street, Klari and I were supposed to split up, but we couldn't bring ourselves to go our separate ways on this awful night. Finally, after a long goodbye, we parted with trepidation. I was told to avoid József Boulevard because it was the most dangerous route. So I made it home, having taken the side streets, sometimes running, sometimes ducking shots or huddling up against strangers. After the previous sleepless night, my family was fast asleep, totally unaware of what was happening. Later that night, we heard shots and wondered, with anxiety, what the coming days would hold for us.

October 24
We saw crowds marching from Baross Street toward the boulevard, amid constant gunfire. At that point we heard the awful news that Russian tanks were rolling through the streets of the capital. This news made the people stop from time to time until they got used to it. In the afternoon, my brother-in-law joined us and told us about the sad things he'd witnessed on the boulevard: there were corpses lying in the street and ambulances constantly rushing about. We were waiting for things to calm down.

October 25
The situation grew more serious. People were standing in line in front of grocery stores, amid a storm of bullets. We began to realize that order would not be restored any time soon. Józsi went to get bread, Ilona went to fetch other groceries, and I stayed home worrying about when I would see them again. There was no news of Tibi, which made the situation doubly unbearable.

October 26
The fighting continued. The air reverberated with constant cannon fire, and in the morning the phone rang, and Ilus cried out, "Tibike!" As if I had been shot out of a cannon I dashed to the phone, and it was indeed him, my dear one. He had been released, but it would have been

too dangerous to come to Pest, and so he remained in Erzsébet. The knowledge that he was free made me very happy. From time to time the tenants in our building went down to the cellar, and we joined them once or twice, but most of the time we considered the apartment safe enough. Yet later on when we saw the devastation, we realized that it had been recklessness on our part.

October 27

The fighting continued. We didn't dare to leave the apartment, and we were so unprepared for this that we were already struggling with food shortages.

October 28

The fighting took on more dangerous proportions. The apartments along the boulevard were bombed out, and we didn't know how long this could go on.

October 29

Even our building was fired at. We were sitting in the blacked-out apartment all day. We didn't find out anything from the radio, and the uncertainty was awful.

October 30, 31

The fighting quieted down, but the street was still deserted. Later we ventured out into the street, and it was terrible to see the results of the destruction everywhere. The mounds of temporary graves were scattered around the playgrounds; there were more orphans. One could still hear sporadic shots coming from different parts of the city. The days were spent relatively quietly, although you could tell that all was not well.

November 3

We feel such joy. Tibi arrived from Erzsébet, and he spent the night with us.

November 4

We were awakened at dawn by the sound of cannon fire; everyone was devastated. On the radio you could hear calls for help in English, French and German, directed to the world, but no help came. I woke up my sweet little children and rushed them down to the cellar. The barrage of gunfire grew more intense, and we were sitting in the cellar, in the dark, hungry and dreadfully afraid. At noon we felt a strong blast, and returning to the apartment was out of the question. The evening was approaching, and it was clear that we had to settle there for the night. Of course there was no way we would sleep, but we made some sort of a bed out of wood for the children. With trepidation, we went upstairs to fetch some bed linen, and sitting on the floor, we waited for the terrible night to begin.

November 5

At dawn we were awakened by the sound of cannon fire and everything continued as before, but I will never forget what happened between twelve and one o'clock. The cellar wall suffered a direct hit, and we were expecting that everything above us would collapse and the cellar would cave in on us. The helplessness was unbearable, there was no way to escape, and we were waiting for the awful end. We were the only Jews in the building and we were on good terms with everyone, but when they started singing hymns during the gunshots, I thought those were sounds from the afterworld. After one o'clock the shots grew more distant, but we could see the signs of the attack everywhere around us. Later on Józsi and Tibi ventured upstairs for a minute and were surprised to see that our apartment remained intact, although I wasn't especially interested in that, because in those tragic hours, my only wish was to come out of the situation alive, and I didn't care about the apartment.

November 6–8

Things remained unchanged; we were sitting in the cellar trembling, and on the morning of the eighth we ventured upstairs for the first time, although one could still hear shooting in the distance. It was awful that we had no news from my father and Klari.

November 9

The situation normalized somewhat and we dared to go out onto the street. The horrible sight that greeted us might have sent us straight back to the cellar, but the lineup for bread began, amid distant cannon fire and nearby tank gun barrels. We roamed the whole district looking for bread, which by now was reduced to half-ration, but usually they ran out just as our turn was coming up. We had electricity again, but what we heard on the radio caused even more anxiety. We found out how many people were trying to leave the country during the upheaval, and on foreign radio broadcasts we listened to the messages from those who'd succeeded, greatly envying them. The long soul-searching began: shall we go or shall we stay? Finally, after many sleepless nights, we made up our minds to leave all we'd achieved in twelve years of struggle and the warmth of home, and we set off with our two small children into the cold and uncertain foreign winter.

December 5

After spending a night at Klari's, the ten of us² sat in the Keleti [Eastern] *Railway Station, waiting for the train leaving for Mosonmagyaróvár. I cannot forget how worried I felt about having our papers checked. We got off two stations before Mosonmagyaróvár. We found ourselves in a completely unfamiliar place, at the mercy of strangers. We were sleeping on some straw spread on the ground, waiting for someone to show us the way the next morning, and be well paid for it. Our*

---

2   Zsuzsanna, her husband, Józsi, and their two children, Peter and Gabi; Zsuzsanna's father, Ervin, and her brother, Tibi; and Zsuzsanna's sister, Klari, her husband, Geza, and their two children, Andrew and Alex.

road led us through the boggy Hanság area, through wind and rain, on deserted roads, avoiding major highways, across a canal on slippery muddy roads, with our father, because even though he didn't want to leave, he took it for granted that he would come with us, though I doubt we would have left without him, and with the four little children. We just kept going. Around two in the afternoon we reached a state farm, where, after a long dispute, one of the employees was willing to transport us by farm wagon to the nearby village of Mosonszentjános, which was our ultimate destination in Hungary.

December 7–31

At dawn, we were taken to Austria by farm wagon, fortunately not encountering any Russian or Hungarian border guards. In a jubilant mood, we were incredulous that we had arrived on Austrian soil. That's how my little Gabi celebrated his 20-month birthday. He arrived in a foreign country, never to remember his little baby carriage, his little crib and the home where he took his first toddling steps. Our first stop in Austria was Andau, where our little Peter's boots were stolen. They were the only thing he had insisted on bringing along. After a whole day on the train, we arrived in Sankt Pölten, where we spent three weeks under rather poor conditions. I don't know if it was the bad provisions or what, but Gabi was very sick; the poor dear couldn't eat and he got so weak that he was not able to stand up. It seemed that in spite of having the boat tickets in our hands, we would need to stay on there, but thank God he recovered, and thus on December 27, we could start our trip to our new destination, Canada. After two in the afternoon we boarded the train in extremely cold weather under uncomfortable conditions; we arrived sleepily the next evening in Bremerhaven. Thus it was that evening that we said goodbye to Europe, which had not afforded us much happiness, yet it was our home, and it hurt that I could not see it in the sunlight one more time, unlike our immediate home in Hungary, to which I had bidden farewell during that last sunset.

Our ship, from the Arosa Line, set sail at dawn, but we were fast asleep at the time, as we couldn't resist our drowsiness. The first day was very pleasant; we got to know the beautiful ship and settled into our small cabin. On December 30, we were awakened by strong waves and stricken by the dreaded seasickness. Although we were reassured that this would only last as long as we were in La Manche [the English Channel], *it stayed with us for the whole of the sea voyage, which lasted eleven days instead of one week.*

January 9, 1957!!

We disembarked in Canada. This was a great day, or rather a great moment, to be on solid ground again. Apart from not feeling well physically, it was depressing that wherever we looked, all we saw was water. We were at the mercy of the elements, and I kept wondering whether we had the right to assume the responsibility for exposing our children to so many dangers, but thank God their young little constitutions stood the test, and in spite of the cold and lack of sleep they arrived healthy in their new country. From the harbour of Saint John, it took us one day of travel to reach Quebec City on January 10. Luckily we spent only five days there. Yet it caused us great sorrow to say goodbye, because as a result of a medical test, our father had to stay behind in the hospital, and Tibike stayed with him. Thus, after a sad goodbye, we arrived in Toronto without them on January 16.

This was the second time we had to start over again, and it was very difficult. We arrived in Toronto without a penny and without knowing the language. But my husband worked as a tailor and I sewed from home for a factory, and we were able to make a good life. After two and a half months, my father was able to leave Quebec City and move to a sanatorium closer to us, so we could visit him. Eventually, he lived with my sister, and then with my family. He passed away in 1967 at the age of seventy-seven. My sister, Klari, sewed in a factory and my brother, Tibi, worked as a tailor for a few years and then became a successful businessman. We all remained very close throughout the years, and we still are.

Unfortunately, I lost my beloved husband, whom I will miss as long as I live, on March 8, 2012, after sixty-two years of marriage. I mourn for Joseph every day, but my husband and I did not survive without a purpose. We survived to leave the next generation, trying to make up for, but not to replace, all those innocent children who never had a chance to grow old.

My two wonderful sons, Peter and David, both live in Toronto with their families, my grandchildren and great-grandson. Peter and his wife, Frances, are the happy parents of Jason, Devorah and Eli. Devorah's son, Aaron Shalom, is our great-grandson. David and Rachel's children are Ariel, Hannah, Jacob and Shoshana Gitel. Being a parent, grandparent and great-grandparent are my biggest rewards and accomplishments.

Many years after we immigrated to Canada, I read my two sons the remnants of my old diary, and they asked me to write my story. So in 1976 I typed out my story in both Hungarian and English for my two sons and now, at eighty-eight years old, I have told my story to you, as I feel it is my duty to keep alive the memory of all the victims who cannot speak for themselves.

I think I survived because it was *beshert*, meant to be. Also, I was with my sister the entire time, and if we hadn't been together, I don't think either of us would have been able to survive. We took care of each other all the time. When one of us fainted or couldn't go on, we helped each other.

It is so very hard to relive the heartache and the horrors and to remember our pre-war life, which I long for but can never find again. I will always cry for my loved ones who never came back. Hitler didn't just put the number A12396 on my arm, but in my heart and in my mind.

My dear departed ones, you are always with me. Rest, my dears. Even though you do not have a grave, you are in heaven.

Epilogue

When I started to write, I was hoping to leave out, completely out, the most tragic part of my life but it is impossible – it will be with me as long as I live.

And I am able to remember.

And when I look back now to my happy childhood and how it was broken in two, it hurts more and more.

1945.

I was almost twenty years old when we came back, and when I look at the twenty-year-olds today, I remember how when I was twenty, I thought I didn't have any future, if I was even thinking at all.

It took me thirty-one years to write about my nightmares for my children; and sometime in 2013, I decided to share them with whoever is interested.

I owe it to the memory of all who disappeared without a grave, to the memory of all the children who never had a chance to grow up, for all the victims who never grew old.

And because there are fewer and fewer witnesses, and even in our lifetime there are those who deny that the Holocaust ever happened.

In my memoir I wrote about the beginning of my life, how I was born into a loving, caring family. With plans for my future, without knowing Hell would break loose.

I won't write again about 1944 or 1945, because I am still living it.

Or because I am hoping to start a new life. I still have nightmares.

I don't have clear memories of the first few years after the war. Maybe my mind wasn't back to normal.

I had my freedom, but it took me awhile to know how to be. I didn't know how to be free again; how was I to live?

I don't remember where we got the first pillow to sleep on, the first bed, or the first plate to eat from, or if there was anything to eat. Like I said, I had to learn how to live again. Like a human being.

1949.

Another milestone in my life. I married my dear husband, Joseph. I had a home again.

1950.

I became a mother to Gyurika, whom we unfortunately lost.

In 1952 our Peter came along, and in 1955, David. Both of them gave us lots of happiness, God bless them.

Then I started to be me again; I had a reason to live – to raise a new generation of Jewish children.

And now, should I say, the final chapter?

November 18, 2015.

I turned NINETY years old. Who would believe it, after all those years of hardship and suffering?

Unfortunately alone, without my loving partner of sixty-two years, whom I will miss forever and for whom I am very grateful. My Józsi and I did everything together – from sewing, to working on a chicken farm in Pickering, to working in a carpet store. We spent twenty-four hours a day together and sadly had only a few peaceful retirement years together.

Thank God I am blessed with my two sons, my seven grandchildren and one great-grandson.

But without Józsi, life will never be the same.

~

A few days ago, I promised myself I would start to write again, which, in my loneliness, is the next best thing, if there is nobody to speak to.

But the problem is that I am going back more and more to the sad, tragic episodes in my ninety-year-old life.

Sometimes I wonder if it is a blessing to have a good memory or not, or if it would be healthier not to remember everything.

But I want to remember.

I wake up during the night and either I don't remember or I don't want to remember what happened yesterday, but, oh yes, I remember what happened then, more than seventy years ago; yes, it is burned into me, into my heart and my whole being as long as I live.

I wrote a lot about it and yet, there are still certain episodes that I left out. Did I ever write about my favourite dress, what I was wearing on the way to Auschwitz? I wonder who was wearing it after – did she know it belonged to somebody else before? Someone who was now wearing men's underwear and a pink garbage … you couldn't call it a dress. Or after a short time, that she was walking barefoot because her shoes didn't last on the unpaved roads?

I am sure I wrote about not recognizing each other without hair, about being bald; C Lager, Saturday, June 3, the first time standing in line, being one in a line of five, being counted.

They were afraid we would escape? We were so valuable to them?

We saw the wire fence, but we didn't know there was electricity in it, just like we saw and were smelling the smoke, but we didn't know what was happening because no human being could ever imagine that people were capable of doing what they did.

In a way I am my own enemy, writing and thinking so much about it, but I just can't help it.

I am sure I will have left out important happenings; when I wake up during the night and everything is coming back, then I should write it all down.

Or maybe not. Who cares?

I am trying not to write more about Auschwitz, for my own sanity, if there is any left.

I am here, living, in my/our past.

Eva Shainblum

I have recorded these words as a message for future generations. I need my son and my daughter to carry this story forward so that it is never forgotten. I have done this for their sake, and now for my granddaughters. The Jewish people should not forget what we went through. Carry it on to the next generation. I only hope that in writing my memoir and telling my story, I haven't caused my family too much pain.

In memory of my beloved husband, Max, and my beloved family who perished in the Holocaust.

Foreword

Eva Shainblum is my inspiration as well as my friend. I am a generation younger, and I often turn to her because of her resilience. I have edited many books and articles about the Holocaust and about antisemitism in Europe, and after hearing Eva's story, I wanted her to write it down. I thank her for her patience, for it took me far longer to assist her than either of us imagined.

Editing a Holocaust memoir is fraught with challenges. The editor needs to probe into areas that are sometimes untouchable. An editor is not a psychologist or social worker, equipped with the words to soothe or move on to another topic. I would find myself at an impasse, wondering with sadness how I would have coped under Eva's circumstances. Eva would describe ordinary events in a family's life, or she would show me a photograph of her siblings, playing with their toys, trusting the world. It was almost impossible for me to record her words. She had more strength than I did. When I read about her relationship with her sister, I thought of my own sister and how fortunate we have been. Eva has, by contrast, lost so many worthy, loving people, and yet carried on to remake her life in Canada.

I am proud to have assisted in editing her memoir. More than anything, I am proud that Eva wrote this book for her children and her beautiful granddaughters. May they learn from her words and her story, just as her friends have learned from her.

Joyce Rappaport

Family Meant Everything

Before the war, I was a happy young girl in the small city of Oradea, Romania. This city, known in Hungarian as Nagyvárad, was famous for its charming river, sense of style and thriving Jewish community of approximately 27,000. It was my home, and I never, ever thought that this would change. I was born there on September 16, 1927, and was named Reizi, after my mother's best friend, though today people call me Eva.

My father, Béla Steinberger, was born in a small town called Csenger, in northeastern Hungary. Later in his childhood, his family moved to Halmi, near the border of Czechoslovakia, where many members of his extended family lived. It was there that he met my mother, Esther Rosenberg, and they fell in love when they were quite young.

Halmi, however, was a town without many opportunities. It lacked industries, and most of its residents worked as border guards, tailors or shoemakers. Others, including Jews, worked in agriculture. My paternal grandfather, Paul, for whom my brother would later be named, had a job as an agricultural inspector. He looked after large farms and travelled between them to see how they were faring.

When my father was very young, he realized how limited his future would be if he stayed in Halmi. He had incredible skills in mathematics – I heard that he could calculate any sum in his head – and he hoped to make a living in the business world. To earn a living, he moved to Budapest, where he picked up the skills to be a merchant. He also served in the Hungarian Army. My father could have had a future in Budapest, a cosmopolitan European city, but he wanted to marry the girl he loved. He dreamed of her, they corresponded and he decided to move back to her town.

There was one problem – not an unusual one in that era. My mother's parents were very religious, but my father was not. Mother's parents were terrified that Béla would lead Esther away from Jewish tradition, so they refused to give my father permission to marry their daughter. This did not stop my parents from loving each other. For years they corresponded, hoping and vowing to one day be together. Finally, my father promised to become more religious and convinced my grandparents to allow their engagement. All in all, it took seven years for them to marry.

A family story is connected to their wedding day. My mother had beautiful black hair, which my father loved very much. However, it was an Orthodox Jewish tradition for women to cut their hair and cover it upon getting married so others would not see it. Still, it was just a custom, and my mother was told by her parents that she would not have to do this. My father certainly did not expect her to cut her hair. But immediately after the wedding ceremony, several zealous old ladies took hold of my mother and cut off almost all her hair. My father was shocked but eventually he came to accept it, and indeed he grew quite religious himself.

After the wedding in 1923, my parents settled in Oradea. At that time, and at the time of my birth, the city was under Romanian rule. The city had a full Jewish cultural network – synagogues, schools of all sorts, a number of youth groups, Zionist groups and Jewish theatres.

Although my father struggled to make a living, he eventually worked as the wholesale distributor for the Rippner Comb Manufacturing Company, also selling combs and other items from a small store. He made an honourable living and was able to provide for us, as well as give to charity and contribute to the welfare of his parents, brothers and sisters. After his own father died, my father made sure that his widowed mother did not live in poverty. One of his sisters also provided for the family, sewing to help their many siblings in their small town. My father's mother, Kathe, died many years before the war.

Sometimes people took advantage of my father because he was so kind. In Europe, long hair was the fashion, and a variety of combs were in style. He would hire salesmen to travel to marketplaces, carrying trunks filled with drawers of merchandise. Sometimes, dishonest workers would tell him that they had been robbed, and my father would feel that he had no choice but to supply them with more items. He was far too trusting; he was a giving person, a mensch. I don't like to say it, but I am relieved that he didn't survive to see almost his whole family killed. With his kind heart, he would not, I am sure, have been able to endure his grief.

I have the most beautiful memories of my father. I adored him with all my being. He was sensitive to everyone's needs, whether people were family or strangers. How fondly I remember his attention to us when we were sick. He would sit at our bedsides in his rocking chair, his warm hand feeling our pulses, remaining all night if we needed him to comfort us. He was kind, and he never had the heart to punish us; he even got upset when our mother, who was the stricter parent, had to discipline us. He and my mother were a loving, respectful couple who brought us up to be compassionate as well.

My mother, the firm one in our family, was informally called Ettu, although her name was Esther. She was born in Halmi in 1898 into a healthy family in which all twelve children survived their childhoods. Only one of her brothers, Matyas (Matthew), did not reach full adulthood; he passed away of asthma at age twenty and is buried in Nagyvárad. Sadly, my mother's father, David Rosenberg, died of blood poisoning when he was only forty-two. Three of my mother's brothers – Sam, Eddie and Sol – and two of her sisters, Lily and Frida, immigrated to the United States before the war, in the late 1920s or early 1930s. One brother, Joseph, went to Palestine in the 1930s. Her other two sisters, Eva and Ilonka, and another brother, Ignatz, perished in the Holocaust. Her brother Alek survived.

Family was always the most important part of our lives. Though we lived in a small house, it was never *too* small. It was always filled with visitors. When our aunts and uncles came to visit, we children would have to go to the neighbour's house to sleep. But those occasions were full of joy. We had other relatives in our city, too, as one of Father's sisters had moved to Nagyvárad from Halmi. We stayed in touch with the others, and travelled by train to visit each other before the war. I learned that, ironically, my maternal grandmother, Dora, had gone to New York when she was a young girl but returned to Halmi and married there. Imagine – we could have all been born in the United States. Instead, my grandmother's fate was to be deported to Auschwitz when she was seventy-four years old.

I was attached to my mother, and I still get upset when I think about a particular incident. Every year, my parents would travel to Halmi to visit the graves of my grandfather and other relatives. The year I was four, I did not want my mother to leave, even though my grandmother took good care of us. I was just a little girl, and I wanted my mother. When the horse-drawn carriage arrived to take my parents to the train, I started to cry and ran after the coach. Because she was concerned about me, my mother turned around, accidentally stepping onto the edge of the vehicle, and fell down into the road. Her face was bruised, and she had a scar from the bleeding. They decided to travel anyway, and the tavern owner at the corner gave her some ice to soothe her injuries. But the image has stayed with me all my life: because of me, my mother was hurt. I still feel the pain of that day. I loved her deeply and miss her with all my heart.

My mother was a hard-working woman who helped my father in his comb-supply business every day. She did this while taking care of us and running a traditional Jewish home. On Thursday nights, after working in the shop all day, she would start her preparations for

Shabbat, kneading the challahs and setting them out to bake on Friday morning. She found the time to bake delicious cakes, helped by my sister and me as we grew older. She also had help from a woman who was hired to wash the clothing, a Hungarian servant named Mrs. Nagy.

We were a family who respected and looked out for each other. I have warm memories of my kind brothers, Paul, who was born in 1924, and David, who was born in 1930. They brought such joy to my parents. My little brother, David, was the best student in the school and often tutored the other children. All I have to memorialize him is a photograph that one of his classmate's brothers gave me in Israel after the war. The picture has David's signature on it. He was a kind, sweet soul.

Paul's teachers, particularly a Mr. Saltzman, were amazed at his brilliance; Paul seemed to have a photographic memory and never had to study long. His schoolteachers came to our home and told us how gifted he was. I remember celebrating his bar mitzvah, first going to the large synagogue to watch him have his first *aliyah*, and then returning to our home with his teachers, the rabbis and our family to continue the celebration.

Paul grew up, succeeded in his education and, at age seventeen or eighteen, helped my father in his business. I will never forget his large, kind eyes. I remember how he helped my maternal grandmother night after night, without complaint, when he was a teenager. My grandmother lived alone in a house deep inside a yard; for years, Paul slept at my grandmother's home, helping her relieve the nightly nosebleeds that were symptoms of her high blood pressure. And on the holiday of Purim, he would volunteer to go to the homes of the sick and elderly and read them the Megillah, since they were unable to travel to synagogue.

And then there was my brave and loyal sister, Ella. She was just two years older than I was, and I idolized her. My mother used to dress Ella and me identically; a dressmaker named Mrs. Berger would come to the house and sew dresses for us. The two of us looked charming in our matching blue skirts and white blouses. And when we got new, identical shoes for the holidays, we looked like twins. We were together all the time, playing, walking to school, helping out in the kitchen and doing our homework in the evening. The two of us attended Jewish schools, first the elementary school – where we learned Romanian or Hungarian, depending on the political situation and on which government was ruling our city – and then the Orthodox high school, where we received both a religious and a secular education. After the regular school day, we girls went to the Bais Yaakov school to continue our Orthodox education. Similarly, our brothers attended yeshiva after the regular school day. We also learned to sew and cook, but my favourite subject was poetry. Unlike my brothers, I did not inherit my father's capability in mathematics.

Outside our cozy home at 7 Liliom Street, a vibrant Jewish community existed. It was a multilingual neighbourhood. We spoke Hungarian, not Yiddish, at home because my mother and father were fluent in Hungarian, as were many of the Jews in our country. Even when the Romanians took over Nagyvárad after the signing of the Treaty of Trianon in 1920 and changed the name of the city to Oradea, our teachers continued to speak to us in Hungarian, though the lectures were supposed to be in Romanian. The school had to import special teachers who knew the language.

Our neighbourhood was almost totally Jewish, and many of the people were Hasidim. Our next-door neighbours, the Geringers, were from Poland. The Geringers had come to Oradea after World War I, to escape the pogroms in Poland in 1918. They were kind, wonderful people. Mr. Geringer had four children from his second marriage and two from his first. One of the little girls had some physical problems; the family never had an easy time. As one of the *gabba'im*, assistants, of the synagogue, Mr. Geringer dedicated his whole life to serving the renowned Vizhnitzer rabbi. He would get up early each morning, proceed to the market and bring supplies to the rabbi's house, despite not being a young man himself.

When the holidays arrived, Mrs. Geringer had to take care of many of the rabbi's followers, who came from far and wide to be with him. She worked hard, cooking and baking. Her children had to give up their beds for the guests. The family also had several young men staying with them who had come to study with the great rabbi, who lived in our neighbourhood.

We were religious but not Hasidic, although we attended services at the Vizhnitzer rabbi's synagogue on Friday nights. Our family always practised Jewish traditions, which was the way most Jews lived in the smaller cities, and I played with children from all sorts of Jewish families. Two sisters, Cirl and Helen, who were very religious, were our good friends, and we took violin lessons together.

Father rose each morning at six, walked to the small synagogue and studied the Torah with his rabbi. Father was a generous, charitable man who would look after the poor, in synagogue and elsewhere. He used to sign promissory notes, help provide dowries for brides and, at a bris, serve as the *kvatter*, a man of honour who carries the baby. He also made sure that each of us children received a proper education in our city's traditional Jewish schools.

On Friday evenings and Shabbat mornings, my father would walk over to the small, poor congregation to pray. Most of the time he would bring numerous guests home for dinner (this, too, was a Jewish tradition). My mother never complained – she knew that the poor people needed the meals more than we did. Mother always prepared more food than our immediate family required, and she joked that she could always add more water to the soup. Even during the week, my father sometimes brought home a hungry person who needed breakfast. When he went to synagogue, he put some money into his pocket to give to charity. My mother sometimes chided him, saying he should leave money for us at home, too.

Our Shabbat meals were scrumptious. After Kiddush over the wine, and after eating huge pieces of challah, we had chicken soup, carp and my mother's true specialty: chicken breasts. On Saturday we had sweet coffee cake and hot *cholent*, a stew that was a standard meal on the Sabbath. The *cholent* was brought in from the communal baking area down the street, since religious Jews could not warm their food at home on the Sabbath. At the bakery, a non-Jew was hired to light the stove. Even at our home, a gentile townsperson made sure that the house was warm and well lit.

We loved the holidays – every one of them. I recall the white tablecloth and candles that adorned our table at Chanukah, Rosh Hashanah and the meal preceding the fast on Yom Kippur. Every Purim, we would bake a huge challah with raisins that seemed three times its regular size, and a delicious turkey stuffed with challah, liver and mushrooms. The whole family, and our neighbours, attended these feasts. So many people in our small house! But it was a house open to everyone.

There were people of all social classes in Oradea. Many in the Jewish community were very well educated and appreciated the cultural activities that the city offered. Actors came from all over the world – often from Budapest and Bucharest – to perform there. My parents were not the type to seclude us from the rest of society. They took us to performances of opera, theatre and other music. We followed the opera libretti in Hungarian. Some of the entertainment was for Jewish audiences; Jewish theatre groups arrived from Poland to perform for us, even though we were not in a large city. At home we had a gramophone, which we wound up with a handle, so we could listen to Jewish recordings as well as other kinds. And to follow the news, we read the local Jewish newspaper and other papers.

We read books, too, lots of books. My sister and I would cover the gap under the door to our room so our parents would not see the light by which we were reading late into the night. The books we read were mostly in Hungarian because our parents did not speak Yiddish very well (my father knew Yiddish better than my mother did). It was also the fashion, before the rise of Hitler and the Nazis, for Hungarian Jewish children to learn German. Ironically, when our parents spoke in Yiddish so that we could not understand them, we could follow their conversation anyway because German is so similar.

We were exposed to many forms of expression, and this included Zionism. The town had chapters of the Zionist organizations Mizrachi and Betar. My mother's brother Joseph was a member of Mizrachi; when he decided to move to British Mandate Palestine in the 1930s, we accompanied him to the railroad station. He was fortunate to be able to leave when he did. My siblings belonged to various Jewish youth groups as well. We stuck together. This helped us deal with the approaching antisemitism.

The New Regime

Throughout the 1930s, we followed the news about Hitler and the Nazis' rise to power. For a long time, these problems seemed quite distant. After all, we were Hungarians, and even when we were under Romanian rule, the situation in Germany seemed far away. In 1938 and early 1939, when we heard about the fall of Czechoslovakia and Austria to the Germans, it seemed irrelevant to us. Everyone said this was not going to happen in Hungary. Most believed it and stayed put. People tend not to believe in danger until it comes to their door. It was very difficult to pick oneself up, to leave everything behind and go. And where was there to go? Other parts of Europe were too dangerous, and America had closed its borders tightly.

We believed that our government would not succumb to Nazi pressure. I was not personally very exposed to the news, because I was a sheltered child in a Jewish neighbourhood, attending Jewish schools. Still, we heard stories. We heard of Jews being beaten and of beards being torn from the faces of Jewish men. I remember a shocking story about a man's long beard being tugged off as he boarded a train. The train door was pulled shut, and his beard was wrenched painfully off his face. We heard more of these stories after the Romanian Iron Guard increased its antisemitic activity in the mid-1930s.

I did not have much contact with non-Jewish children. The only non-Jews I talked to were the servants in our house or the occasional person at my father's business. I did not personally experience anti-Jewish acts, and as a young adolescent I could go about my life and put the worries into some other part of my mind.

Before the Germans arrived, the Hungarians had again taken our city from the Romanians, in August 1940. That was supposed to be a joyful time. Indeed, I had never seen my father so elated. He had always been so grateful to Hungary, the country in which he had served in the army and had learned his trade. When he heard that the Hungarians were returning, he was thrilled. He actually stood out on the street, waiting for them. When the leader, Miklós Horthy, passed by on a white horse, my father was ecstatic. He told us how life was finally going to change, that there would be no antisemitism. But what he did not realize was that Hungary was a completely different country. In this new Hungary, my father would lose this happiness, as well as his life and his family. As reality set in, he never forgave himself for having felt so ecstatic.

In the beginning of the new regime, things seemed fine. But as the war progressed in other parts of Europe, antisemitism flourished, affecting not just the general atmosphere but people in their daily dealings with everyone in the non-Jewish community. We were the scapegoats; anyone with money trouble or hunger immediately blamed the Jews. Anti-Jewish laws were soon imposed. Jews were forced to give up their livelihoods, and stores and businesses were taken over by non-Jews. Restrictions became a reality that we had to suffer through. I remember that we could not attend theatres or be admitted to universities.

When pogroms started in Eastern Europe, Jewish refugees from Poland and the Soviet Union arrived in Oradea. One day my father risked his life warning our neighbours that the authorities were searching for illegal newcomers. The Jewish refugees were the first victims after Hungary entered the war, allied with Germany, in June 1941. Our neighbours the Geringers, too, suffered greatly from the realistic fear that foreign Jews who lacked citizenship would be the first to be deported. Early one morning, we heard banging on the neighbours' door. We ran over to the yard and saw soldiers coming to pick up the people they called foreigners. We lived in the corner house, and there was a fence with great wide slats between our house and the Geringers' house. There was also a gate on the other side of our house. My father was anxious to save the Geringers, and he opened the gate so that they could get through, risking his life in the process. They escaped into our yard through two loosened slats, then from our corner house through a back door. The authorities didn't see them, but they were deported later on. Not one of them survived.

At that somewhat early point, my father began to think of leaving Hungary for Romania. Although my father was not a Hasid, he trusted the Vizhnitzer rabbi and asked him for his opinion. In response, the rabbi said, "Wait. The time is not yet ripe. I will tell you when it is time to leave."

On March 19, 1944, the Germans took over our city, and there was no way to escape. We started to become frantic. Each day, we saw worse acts of violence. By the beginning of April, we had to wear the yellow star. We felt terrible, standing out from the crowd, marked as targets for antisemites. One was lucky not to get beaten up. Many young men had been taken into the forced labour service of the Hungarian army. The men in my immediate family were spared this, as my father was too old and my brothers were too young. But one of my uncles, Jenö Steinberger, was sent to the labour service. He had arrived from Romania to be "safe" with his family. Later on, his whole family perished in Auschwitz.

Less than two months after the occupation, in collaboration with the Germans, the Hungarian authorities ordered all the Jews into a crowded ghetto. We did not have to move, as our house was already located in the ghetto area. The living conditions in the ghetto were horrendous. Non-Jews had to move out, and Jews from other parts of the city were forced to move in with us. Many families came to share our small house. There was not enough space for us all – every inch was occupied. Food was very scarce, and people subsisted on what they had hoarded before the ghetto was formed. Coming from a wonderfully sheltered life, I found this unbelievably sad. We had no idea of what would happen next, and even though we heard rumours from other parts of Europe, they seemed so outlandish that we forced ourselves not to believe them. All we wanted was to be together, but not together like this. We could not get out. Gendarmes stood at the entrances, making escape impossible.

We were subject to curfews, food shortages and humiliating restrictions. My father's business had disappeared, of course, and we could barely get by. Just before the war, our economic situation had improved, but ultimately my father's success meant nothing. It was too late – who could think of buying combs and accessories? Our city had been called "Small Paris," a place of distinction and elegance. It was ironic and cruel that we were banded together in a repulsive ghetto.

My brother Paul was determined to flee, and he begged my father to grant him permission to go somewhere perceived as safer. Paul was the only one intelligent enough to predict the future of the Jews in our town. Paul told my father that we were in immense danger, that the news from other parts of Europe was an indication of what was to come. He cried, "If you let me go, at least one of us will survive to carry your blood to future generations." Father reluctantly gave Paul his permission. That same night, the Vizhnitzer rabbi and his family, along with many of the rabbi's followers, attempted to escape to Romania. Paul joined them. The group paid a lot of money to a smuggler who led them underground through the sewer system. Unfortunately, the guards caught my brother and many others and brought them back to the Nagyvárad ghetto, to the great synagogue, our place of sanctuary, which they had turned into a prison. Paul remained there until the trains deported us all. Our friend Helen was arrested at the same time as my brother. She was tortured but survived the war, as did her sister, Cirl.

Above all, I remember feeling fearful. The police and gendarmes wore terrifying uniforms with rooster plumes in their hats. I would literally shiver when I saw them coming. We watched what we said and tried not to make our presence obvious. Still, how could we hide? The Hungarians, and later the Germans, did not need a reason to make trouble for Jews; our mere existence seemed to give them the justification to hurt and torture us.

We were humiliated and dehumanized each day. The Hungarian gendarmes followed Nazi orders, rampaging through our streets, picking up people and demanding our valuables. They built a torture chamber in what used to be a beer factory. They would grab Jewish men, take them to be tortured and force them to reveal where their possessions were hidden. One morning, they grabbed my father and tortured him.

The gendarmes came to our house and demanded our valuables. They pulled my mother's wedding ring from her finger; she had been too proud to hide it. They also ruined a treasured gift that my sister and I had recently received. Our birthdays were in the same month, and in 1943 our parents had given us our first watches. When the guards banged on our door in the ghetto, we pulled off the lovely watches, smashed them hard and threw them into the fire. There was no way that I would give them up to the antisemites. After the war, my relatives gave me a photograph of us wearing the watches.

Our schooling had ended when the ghetto started. We were deprived of education, while our parents and all Jews were denied the right to run businesses and stores. I don't know how we bought food – perhaps the grocery stores were able to sell whatever was left. My parents did not want to burden us with frightening details. My father was sensitive and cried all the time when he saw what was happening to us. He had no answer. Nobody did. It was a tragedy that we had not expected. But who could have known that despite our current conditions, worse things were still to come?

My Life Force

As the month of May neared its end, we learned that we would be deported. I later learned that between 25,000 and 38,000 Jews, which included those from areas surrounding Oradea, were sent to Auschwitz. Street by street, our city was depleted. Family by family, our friends disappeared.

During the festival of Shavuos, we knew these would be our last days in our home. Nonetheless, we followed Jewish tradition and did our best to create our final dairy lunch. We had a goat we used to milk to feed the children; somehow the goat produced enough milk for us to "celebrate." The Germans could take away our synagogues, but they could not make us give up religion in our home. We prayed and sat down for what was to be our last meal together. I will never forget that day, and each year on that day, in synagogue, I honour and remember my family's courage in the face of what was to follow.

The next day we were packed into freight trains, trains that were meant for cattle. The Hungarian gendarmes with their rooster feather plumed hats – my nightmare – pushed us into what would be the last journey for so many. Germans then took over the trains. I remember that my sister and I were wearing beautiful, new, high-laced shoes that our father had ordered for us. The shoemaker had told us that everyone should have a place to store some money, and he had created false soles where funds could be hidden. But the Germans threatened to shoot us if they found valuables in our possessions. Out of fear, we tore off the soles and gave them the money.

The guards told us, in a mocking tone, that we were "going on a trip," but no one would tell us where. The anxiety of not knowing drove some people insane. We were terrified, not knowing where we were going. Crammed into the train, we had no place to sit or rest. Religious men who had never seen a woman's body were in a space with a big pot in the middle for bathroom facilities. No curtain, no privacy. People were petrified, hysterical, crying. My brother Paul tried to preserve people's sanity by shielding those who had to relieve themselves, giving them privacy. The wagon was stifling and the odour of excrement and urine was disgusting. Every time the train stopped, the Germans entered and shouted that people better give up everything they had or they would shoot us all inside. We kept only what we were wearing.

Our whole family, including my grandmother, managed to stay together. We had been permitted to bring one little suitcase with clothes. I remember I had just knitted a sweater for myself. I was wearing it, and we had even taken a picture of it before the deportation. I loved that sweater and did not want to give it up. But on the train I tore it up in rage. My mind is a jumble recalling this trauma. The journey took three or four days; I was so scared that it was impossible to gauge the time.

No water except when we left. Nothing on the way. Hunger. People were in a panic, upset, sick. When we stopped we could not see anything; there was a little window up on the top of the train compartment, but the Germans blocked the ladder there, and we could see nothing. The heat was unbearable. There was just enough room to stand, or maybe sit on the floor. Grandparents fainted, and some people hallucinated.

We arrived at Auschwitz on June 1, probably in the morning. I was disoriented, but I remember daylight. Light, but it was the beginning of the longest day of my life. The first thing I saw when we got out of the train was a German man in uniform who kept on yelling "Left!" and "Right!" ordering people where to go: old or incapable of working to one side, young and stronger to the other. My mother, grandmother and youngest brother were separated from us. My mother was holding on to both of them. My grandmother was seventy-four years old, my brother David just fourteen. They were led off in one direction, and I never saw them again.

My sister, my father, Paul and I were sent to the other side. Then my father and Paul were pushed back another way. We had no idea what this division signified and wondered where we were. Who were the strange, emaciated people we had seen when we were taken from that train? Were they Jewish prisoners of war? Why were they gathered around the platform, staring at us from behind the fence? We said to each other, "This must be an insane asylum!"

I whispered to my sister and to anyone else around us, "Where are we?" People were running to the gate, yelling names at us as if they hoped we would answer, hoping we would be related to them. We couldn't understand what was going on. These did not look like civilized human beings.

The guards took us to a vast room, telling us to get undressed because now we were going to be given new clothes. Then they started shaving our hair, and gave us one item of clothing each – a slip or a dress, one or the other. We were confused, enraged. We were allowed to keep our shoes, but Ella and I had torn off the soles, so the shoes were difficult to walk in and of little use.

I felt humiliated. Try to imagine the shame I felt as a protected, religious young woman; hair sheared from my head and pubic area, which were sprayed with disinfectants. I think that this is the worst thing that can happen to a human being – deprived of everything and everybody that we had, we then had to walk around naked in front of the Germans. When they were done they inspected us again, sending away those who were not to their liking. Where were they sending them, I wondered. We started to hear rumours of gas chambers. After the selection, I saw my father and Paul on the other side of the lineup, for a minute or two. They were waving at us, one last time.

My sister and I were sent to the C Lager, where every day the Nazis randomly selected human beings for life or for death. We had become those people we had seen at the arrival point, shaven, wearing rags. In the C Lager were not just our group from Hungary, but other Jews from Eastern Europe: Poles, Czechs, Slovaks and others. All of us were pushed around by guards, including Jewish guards, supervisors called kapos and *Blockälteste*. The guards were mostly Slovaks – tough women who were cruel, whose job it was to keep order. They thought only about their own survival and took their aggression out on us.

My sister and I were assigned to Block C-13, which, relatively speaking, appeared to be a "decent" block, with bunk beds. But it was crowded and unhygienic; twelve people shared one bunk, with no pillows, no blankets, no covers. There were just plain, hard wooden bunks. It was warm now, but how would we survive in winter? Every morning at 5:00 a.m. we were forced to wake up and face a new day of terror, of not knowing what would happen next.

Among us, though I did not know this yet, was our pregnant cousin, Lily. She was in her ninth month, but somehow the guards hadn't noticed and she hadn't been grouped with other pregnant women, who were immediately sent off to the gas chambers. My cousin was tiny and she looked fat, not pregnant. People huddled up against each other and they shielded her pregnancy. On our second day, in this horror, my cousin quietly – how could she have done this quietly? – gave birth to a baby. The *Lagerälteste* suffocated the baby. Lily survived.

We had no choice but to follow the orders of the guards. Every morning we stood to be counted, but we didn't know the purpose of this counting. Later I learned that they were looking us over to choose who would be selected for work camps. After a short while, we knew exactly what the selection was for. We would stand there terrified, wondering whether we would be chosen for a work camp or the gas chambers. On our first day, the *Blockälteste* had said cruelly, "See the chimney smoking there? That could be your parents burning." We had laughed at her, not wanting to believe it. Surely she was making this up. Then, later on, we found out that she was right.

A while after we arrived, we found out that one of our aunts, my father's sister Lenke Fogel, was in Block 30. We moved to that area, glad to be with her. There were no bunks in this section and people slept on the dirt floor. We were "fortunate" that other members of our family were in that camp, including a cousin of my mother's who had four sisters. The family connections were very comforting to us, but we worried every day that we'd get sent away.

The *Blockälteste* there was a beautiful woman with an ugly nature. Two girls from my city served as helpers at the door. One of them told us that she was from a poor family. "At home you were the big shots," she said, "but here, we are." She hit me with a cane.

The women who served as *Blockälteste* had privileges. They were not routinely shaved and their hair was growing back. These women had been deported years earlier, and they had had to be tough to survive. Their attitude toward those of us who had just arrived from Hungary was that we were the lucky ones. They resented the "good" years of freedom that we had had while they were already imprisoned.

Every morning, a beautiful SS woman took us into a field for counting. We stood in line for hours, in terror, knowing what our fate could be. Meanwhile, she stood there almost elegantly – gorgeous, blond, slim, her hair fixed in a bun – with her snarling German shepherd. I can't stand German shepherds even today. People were selected to live or to die. The ill were taken to the gas chamber. But we were all ill – how could one not be under those conditions? As she counted us, she would order the dog to bite any prisoner whom she didn't like, who was standing crooked or who was standing outside the borders of the lines. She also had a whip and would hit us. I do not remember her name.

I remember there was a young man from home who was allowed in our section to clean the toilets. He was from a very religious family, but now he was sent from the men's block to clean the women's bathroom. The only contact between men and women was through him, as the men's camps were far away. This young man risked his life bringing notes from husbands, brothers. *Have you seen my brother? My father?* Once, he told me he had seen my brother before the selections.

There was an inhuman stench at Auschwitz. Not enough water for washing, and no soap. There was no sanitation, and we were full of lice. Food was a little soup, a slice of bread a day, and people stole from each other.

We heard that some children were selected for medical experiments, and that some women were abused. Our womanhood was literally taken away from us. Before the war, I had begun to menstruate. In the camp, it was said that the Nazis added medications to the soup to stop our periods, but I'm not sure if that was true, and it has never been proven.

At one point I developed pneumonia and could do little beyond sleep. During the selections, to save my life, people held me up. My sister, especially, was my life force. We protected each other. My sister had managed to hold on to her glasses – the guards did not take them away – and this was forbidden. I hid them, though every day we were afraid that the guards would find them. We would put them under our armpits, breasts. There was no place to hide items on the floor; there were no covers, no places to stash food.

We kept ourselves alive with jokes and with stories about the food we would devour when we were liberated. Did we really believe that there would be a good ending, that we would be rescued? I don't think so, but we sang and performed for each other anyway, reciting recipes, chanting poetry, trying to cheer each other up. We tried to mask our worries about who would be separated; we grieved for those who were sent to the gas chambers after the daily selections. We watched lice-ridden friends sicken and be carried out by the truckload when they died. If they died during the night, they were taken away by other Jews; men came with carriages to roll them out on wheelbarrows.

~

On October 5, 1944, my sister and I were selected by the SS during a count. We were marked to be sent to a work camp. About sixty of us, including my aunt Lenke and my cousin Dina Hammerstein, were taken to a cattle train. My sister and I were just happy to be together. The train moved day and night, and finally stopped at Camp Mittelsteine in Lower Silesia.

It was a fenced work camp, and from there we had to walk for what seemed like miles to work at a munitions factory. We were assigned to a clean block and were given new rags and wooden shoes. We each had our own bunk bed, rather than one for twelve people. No pillows, of course, but a measure of room. It seemed better than Auschwitz. Anything would have seemed better. But it was just another facet of hell. We had to start work at 6 a.m. It was winter, and we had no coats, no stockings, just uncomfortable clogs, and we marched each day to the factory where we worked at machines, cutting chips for airplanes. Frostbite sores developed on my legs; I still have the marks.

One day, I accidentally broke my sister's glasses, making it impossible for her to work in the factory. I will always feel guilty about this, because her health and strength worsened. She was forced to work outside that winter with my aunt and cousin, digging ditches and trenches.

In Mittelsteine, I became one of the favourite prisoners of an SS woman, a vicious, malicious guard who claimed to like me and said I was pretty. Wanda was her name. She did appear to favour me and would make sure that I was sometimes given extra rations of bread. We had one cup that we were supposed to carry with us all the time, from a string on our belt. Somehow, I broke my cup. And then Wanda, the woman who supposedly liked me, told me that I was to be hanged for that. I was taken outside to where a noose was set up, and she put me under it. I was an innocent young girl, but they wanted to scare me just for breaking a cup. Wanda had a few favourites, pretty girls. When the war was over, some of these girls were said to have helped her get out of Germany. I don't know if this is true, because I did not stay in that camp. I was transferred to another camp that winter.

At the end of April 1945, as Allied troops neared our camp, the Germans moved us to Mährisch Weisswasser, a forced labour camp in the Sudetenland. We had been transferred because the armies were getting closer, and the Germans kept pushing people farther and farther away from the front. But I also remember that the day the armies were getting closer, the Germans told us that we were going to be blown up and that they had put dynamite around the camp. We were told to say our prayers because the SS was going to blow us up, along with all the other evidence of their atrocities.

Thankfully, soon after, Soviet troops arrived, and we were liberated. Freedom. Freedom.

The Long Road Home

On May 8, 1945, the gates of the camp were thrown open, after days of unrest and uncertainty. We were told that the war was now over. Over, but what did that mean for us? It never truly ended for me, and the months and years that followed brought additional tragedies to me and my family.

But on that spring day, Soviet soldiers greeted us, telling us that we were free to leave. But where were we to go? My sister and I were dumbfounded, and we stayed exactly where we were. We were weak and sickly; I weighed only some sixty pounds at that point. The day we were liberated, people were anxious to leave, and they began to steal food and clothes from the neighbouring Germans. But we waited for food to come to us. Much too weak to travel, we chose not to join the other survivors who immediately ran to the nearest village to search for food. We waited a few hours, staying alone and hoping that someone kind would discover us and bring us something to eat and some clothing to wear. Unfortunately, our "rescuers," the Soviet Army, did not care to assist us.

Slowly, we started moving. We went into an empty house and picked up some clothes, including a sweater. Our intention was to go home. So we carried our few belongings in a makeshift bundle with two handles, one for my sister and one for me. No one knew what to do or where, ultimately, to travel. We joined some of the other people from the camp, seeking shelter. Luckily, this group included the woman who had been in charge of our room in the camp, our *Stubenälteste*. We stopped to rest each night, but whenever we arrived somewhere, at a school or a centre, rumours abounded that Soviet soldiers were looking for women to rape, and that they did not care if we were sick or half dead. They didn't care about us and didn't look after the sick. By contrast, we were told that the Americans fed and looked after the ill refugees, and provided medication. The Soviets only looked after their own pleasures. We did not rest well, terrified of being targeted by Soviet soldiers.

One evening, we came upon an empty school building and gratefully tried to settle down. During the night, the Soviet troops came. Our very brave *Stubenälteste* stood outside the entrance, trying to protect us girls; we were all young and frightened. She was gang-raped by the soldiers. She almost died in saving the rest of us. I will never forget her sacrifice. I never found out what happened to her after that.

The next day my sister and I started walking again in the direction of Hungary, toward the home that could never truly be our home again. Sometimes we were able to get a short ride, but most of the trip was by foot. My poor sister was not feeling well, and getting weaker and weaker, but we were so afraid of the Soviets that we both insisted on continuing the journey. At one point, we were able to get on a train for a short time, but there, too, the soldiers boarded, asking for money, watches and girls. We walked and walked, sometimes finding assistance. Some Germans gave us lifts in their hay wagons, drawn by donkeys. Still, no place was safe, not for two young women travelling alone.

Finally, after three weeks, we arrived home. No one from our family was there. The remnants of the Jewish community came together, putting the homeless up in the hospital and other centres. Just as I began to dream of the end of the horror, it became clear that my sister was getting sicker, weakened by all that she had been through. She went to the doctor and was told that she had scarlet fever. Soon after, one of my uncles, Alexander Rosenberg, known as Pityu, came home and had my sister taken to the hospital for contagious diseases, where she was far away and isolated. Worst of all, she was in quarantine, and for the first time since our deportation, we were separated.

That was the most terrible, agonizing event in my life, and in hers – worse, even, than Auschwitz. In the hospital they shaved her head again; that must have been devastating to her. How could they do that to a young woman who had been so humiliated in a death camp? I went every day to the windows of the hospital, but the staff would not let me into the building. That was my life every day, standing at the window.

Life grew a little less bleak when my aunt Lenke, from whom I'd been separated in Weisswasser, came back to Oradea and moved into her home. I left the centre for refugees, where I had been staying, and moved in with her. My own former home had been claimed by our housekeeper – this was painful, but I didn't have the energy or time to care, as I was so preoccupied with my sister.

Within a few weeks, I realized that there was no hope for her survival. Even more tragic was the doctors' discovery that they had misdiagnosed her and were treating her with the wrong medication. She had typhus, not scarlet fever. At that point she was no longer contagious, so they sent her home to my aunt's house. A few days later she died in my arms. It was a Friday morning, August 24. Two hours later, my uncle Alex took her away to be buried. I could not go with her to the cemetery. And there she remains, far away, alone in the land of our birth, the land of our destruction.

In a soup kitchen in Oradea, soon after the end of shiva for my sister, I ran into a young man who had been our neighbour. He told me that he had witnessed my brother Paul's death. He had been killed on the day before liberation. The news shattered any hope that I had. The pain in my heart was unbearable. I knew that there was no chance I would see any other member of my family alive. I had been so sure that my brother would survive: he was young, strong and healthy. I later met a young man who said that Paul had carried a picture of my sister and me during the war, showing it to everyone and talking about his beautiful sisters.

At the end of 1945, my aunt Lenke talked about moving to Cluj, a beautiful city nearby, where Jews had lived for centuries. As I did not want to be alone, I left with her. People started to rebuild their lives, finding consolation in marrying and starting new families. My best friend in Oradea, Adele, had an aunt who married my ex-uncle Herman after the war. In Cluj, Lenke married, as did one of my cousins.

In Cluj, my girlfriend's fiancé, Alex, introduced me to his friend Tibi Goldberger. We met Tibi at a swimming pool and I soon became friends with him and his brothers. After a few months, we started going out. Tibi's family was determined to leave Cluj for Germany. Only from Germany could one hope to find a way out of Europe. Tibi refused to go without me. I didn't want to leave him either, so I accompanied him and his family, along with my cousin Zsofi, who had also lost her parents. The Goldbergers had a relative who had a high position in the US Army, and he promised to help. Unfortunately, bureaucracy moved slowly. Still, we decided to move west to make leaving more possible. The family rented a bus, since there were many of us. I had managed to get back my house in Oradea, so I sold it and used the funds to purchase a memorial stone for my sister. And then I left, taking just my coat and a few small items.

We took the bus to a border town near Hungary where my mother had grown up. At night, we crossed into Hungary by foot. The Soviet and Romanian guards chased us, but we managed to elude them, and from there we took a train to Budapest, where Tibi had a friend. We then got to another border town and walked across the border into Austria, chased again by soldiers. It was psychologically very hard to cross into Germany, the land soaked with Jewish blood.

Tibi's family was able to rent a very nice house; they stayed together and registered to immigrate to the United States. To increase their chances, they also registered with the consuls in other cities. Tibi went to Stuttgart, renting an apartment there with his brother and taking turns staying by the phone in case the consul called.

Meanwhile, I stayed at a series of displaced persons (DP) camps. At first, I was in a DP camp in Vienna, a receiving camp for people from all over the world. From there I was shipped to Salzburg, and then to Munich, and eventually to Landshut, a terrible tent camp where I slept on an army cot. As if this were not enough, from there I was sent to another camp in Kassel, Germany, a city that had been completely bombed out. Not a single house was untouched. I stayed in crowded, unsanitary army barracks. The rations were meagre, but Tibi continued to look after me. He would sometimes travel twenty hours by train to see me, appearing on the steps with parcels of food from his parents. One of my friends, Bea Wiesel, sister of the writer Elie Wiesel, worked for the UNRRA, the United Nations relief organization, and she was able to get us a little extra food.

Bea met a group of Hungarian musicians who played for the Americans, and they said that they could get us a bombed-out house in the city of Kassel to live in. Four of us girls, including my cousin Zsofi, and two boys lived together in this hovel. We had the upstairs, while some other refugees lived downstairs. It, too, was a gruesome place. The house had only one standing outside wall, and inside, there were no dividing walls; instead, we hung blankets to divide the men's and women's areas. No food or heat was supplied, so we had to go to the army barracks for sustenance. At night we went out to steal wood from bombed-out homes to make fires so that we could cook oatmeal. I remember eating mostly oatmeal and ketchup for a few months.

Tibi met a man in Waldheim who was the director of a refugee camp and could assist people who wanted to emigrate. The director told us about a group of child orphans who were heading to Canada. I managed to register and was able to become part of the group along with my cousin Zsofi. Excited to leave Europe behind, we went to the international children's camp in Prien, Bavaria, to prepare. Zsofi eventually went to Australia.

And then, so soon after the death of my sister, tragedy struck once again. One day at the camp someone asked me if we had heard that one of the Goldberger boys had died in an accident. He did not know which one. My heart stopped. I knew right away that it was Tibi. The apartment in Stuttgart, where Tibi had been staying, was heated by gas. The authorities usually turned off the gas from midnight until six in the morning, but hadn't this one time. He had forgotten to close the vent before falling asleep and was suffocated by the fumes. We were supposed to get married as soon as we settled down somewhere. His family had kept the news from me, not wanting anything to keep me from emigrating.

A New Generation

I arrived in Canada on January 13, 1948, when the US Army ship *General S.D. Sturgis* docked in Halifax. Our group then proceeded by train to Montreal, arriving at Central Station. Some of us were continuing to other cities, but my destination was Montreal. We rode in sleeping cars, and those wintry nights through the eastern Canadian countryside were my first comfort in many years.

At Central Station, we were greeted by many people, including Mr. David Weiss, executive director of the Baron de Hirsch Institute and the Jewish Child Welfare Bureau. There were a number of people from various Jewish organizations. Afterwards, we were taken to the Jeanne Mance reception centre, where we stayed until social workers were able to find us lodging and then jobs. The social agencies gave us warm clothing, as we had brought nothing suitable from the DP camps. The group I was with stayed together. We were like family. None of us had any relatives in Montreal, so we formed close friendships and relied on each other.

At the station, I met a very nice couple, the Taveroffs, who immediately invited some of us to their home for Shabbat dinners and holidays. Ida Taveroff took us to stores and to factories, where we received clothing donations. The Taveroffs owned a wedding gown factory and gave us gowns when any of us eventually married. They lived in the same house for sixty-five years, and I stayed in touch with Ida for the rest of her life, visiting her at the Maimonides Home for the Aged until 2003, where she died at the very old age of 101.

My social worker found me a room with a kind Jewish family, the Weinsteins. Their daughter, Gitel (Trudy), was around my age, and we have remained friends. The Weinsteins allowed me to invite my friends over for get-togethers in their home. I gradually felt like I was part of a family again.

The social worker also found me a job at the Lawrence Sperber clothing factory, one of the best fashion enterprises in the city. I learned to be a finisher and also helped the models in the showroom. I was very fortunate to be working at that factory. The workers liked me and made me copies of any dress that I liked. The boss provided the material, the cutter shaped it, the operator sewed it and the presser pressed it. I felt like one of the best-dressed refugees in Montreal. I lived in a poor area of town, and when I walked down the street I could hear people whispering. They were wondering where this refugee girl got her elegant clothes!

After a few months, one of the models I assisted, who was Hungarian, said that she and the owner wanted to train me to be a model, too. But I was shy and not very sophisticated, so I didn't accept the offer. I didn't like the idea of people coming in and out of the showroom while the models were changing their clothes.

I worked in the factory for two years, from 1948 to 1950. My English was improving, so I decided to enroll at a business college to learn bookkeeping. That same week, one of my friends who was working at Lindor, the lingerie chain, told me that she was leaving her job. Right away, I applied for her position, as I wanted to work in an office. I went for my interview and took the job even though the salary was half of what I was earning in the factory. I started as an inventory clerk, and the buyer would ask me to model some of the merchandise that salesmen brought in.

I stayed there until 1952, travelling every morning by bus. I always met the same passengers at the bus stop on the corner, and we would talk to each other while waiting. One woman asked me to consider working for her as an assistant bookkeeper. Because I was taking a course in the field, I happily accepted her offer. I worked with her until 1955. When she got married, I took over her bookkeeping job, and that marked the beginning of my new career.

In the mid-1950s, the company went bankrupt, and I had to apply for unemployment insurance. But when I went to the office to submit the paperwork, they told me of another bookkeeping job for which I had to interview. I had to travel two hours each way, but there was no alternative. I wouldn't get my insurance unless I went for the interview.

The job turned out to be in a very nice French-Canadian firm that owned several flour mills; they exported all over the world and dealt with foreign currency. I told them that I was unqualified for the position, but they really wanted me and said they would teach me all I had to know. The general manager offered me a very good salary as head bookkeeper and would not take "no" for an answer. So I had to accept the position.

Later I found out that they had wanted me because they had had a Jewish bookkeeper who had been very good at the job. It actually turned out to be an excellent position, worth all the hardships of travelling to work. They treated me with the greatest respect. After a few months, I became very ill, and they continued to pay my salary for three months, even though they had to hire a replacement. I was very thankful. Because of them, I was able to pay my hospital bill.

After giving up the position in 1957, I went to live in Toronto, as I was not getting along with my aunt Lenke, with whom I had been living. My dearest friend Adele (Gaga) lived in Toronto and asked me to come and stay with her family. She lived in a large house and said I could stay there until I decided what to do next. I worried about going there; I was afraid that our friendship would suffer. But this did not happen. We became closer than ever. Her children loved me, and I loved them very much, too. Her daughter Rochelle, who was then four years old, came into my room every morning to wake me with a kiss. She's a mother and grandmother herself now, and I still love her. Her brother, George, was a bit older, and I love him, too. They were like my own children in those years.

I had been living in Toronto for about ten months when my friend Bea called, asking me if I wanted to travel to Israel with her. We first went to Paris, where her sister, Hilda, and brother, Elie, were living. In Israel, I toured both Tel Aviv and Jerusalem, and I had a very interesting trip.

In November 1958, I moved back in with my aunt Lenke and my uncle Moritz. I was broke and had to find work, so I stayed with them. In Montreal, my uncle played cards with some of his friends from back in Cluj, Hungary. One man, Mr. Fogel, would get a ride there with his friend Max Shainblum, who was a co-worker. Mr. Fogel knew me slightly, and he wanted Max to meet me. He bothered Max so much about this that Max called me up, and we had a blind date in December 1958.

We fell in love and were married on September 24, 1959, a date we chose because it was my late sister's birthday. We had a small ceremony at a rabbi's office. We started a new life together, and for thirty-eight years we were a loving couple, showing one another affection and respect. In his youth, Max hadn't been able to go to McGill University because of the quota system for Jews, and he never forgave McGill for that. Instead, he went to Queen's University in Kingston. That's where he was when he received word that his father was dying, and though he rushed back to Montreal to be with him, his father had passed away. Max's father died at the young age of fifty, and Max, a loyal son to his widowed mother, became her sole support. Though education was his goal, he took time out for his mother, working one year and going to school the next so that he could earn a living, as she was never able to work. After we married and had a home, Max would pick up his mother on Friday nights to spend the weekends with us. I loved and respected her very much. She loved our children with all her heart – they brought her great pleasure. She lived to a very old age, and Max took care of her until the end of her life.

Max and I rented an apartment on Linton Avenue in Montreal, and we were very happy. Two years later I gave birth to a little girl whom we named Esther, after my mother and my sister. I cannot describe how it felt to have a child of my own. I was able to fulfill my brother's wishes and carry the family genes to the next generation, after having lost all of my own family. When they put Esther into my arms, it was a miracle for me. Two years later, in April 1963, we had a boy, whom we named Mark. His Hebrew name is in honour of my father and my husband's father. He was a sweet child with very blond curly hair, whom everyone adored. Max was always there for me when the children were young. I perpetually worried about them, but he always calmed my fears. We were a good team and had a good marriage.

Esther grew up to be a smart, talented artist. After graduating from McGill University, she studied law at Osgoode Hall in Toronto and received her master's degree from Dalhousie University in Halifax. She moved to Toronto and worked for large law firms and the government of Ontario, where she was a special adviser to the health minister. Now she lives in Ottawa and works for the Victorian Order of Nurses as director of corporate support and general counsel. She is married to Irv Wasserman, and they have a daughter, Noa Michaela.

Mark graduated from Concordia University as a writer, and from McGill University as a teacher. He wrote a comic book called *Northguard*, and when the government issued a stamp of Canadian superheroes, his character was one of them. He also published a book and series called *Angloman*, which was on the bestseller list for two years. Mark is married to Andrea Lobel, a very smart woman who worked as an allergy consultant while completing her doctorate. Their little girl, Maya Gabriella, is named after my husband, whom we lost in 1998, and my sister. My only wish is for our children to have the happiness that Max and I found together.

May 4, 1998, the day that I lost my beloved husband, was one of the saddest days of my life. Though I am very grateful for the years we had, I had always hoped that we would grow old together, walking hand in hand, as we always had done, even just to the corner. He was my strength, my love, my very best friend and my lover, everything that a woman and a wife needs. Most of all, he was a strong and remarkable father to our children, never too tired or too busy to take them where they had to go, even in the middle of the night. He was a role model to our children; they learned to be menschen, just as he was. Just as he read all the time, so did they. His friends called him a walking encyclopedia, and they learned so much from him. He was our backbone, our idol.

Even those who knew Max just slightly felt his kindness. As a professor at Concordia University for more than twenty-five years, he influenced his students and gave his time to teach English to newcomers. Max helped everyone who needed assistance. When my uncle Moritz was very sick, it was Max who took him to the emergency room many nights.

When Max was diagnosed with leukemia it was just before we planned to leave for Europe to visit my sister's grave in Oradea, and his doctors worried about a problem they had found on one of his lymph nodes. But he still wanted to go with our family to visit my hometown and my beloved sister's grave. He never wanted to disappoint me. We enjoyed being together as a family. Visiting the cemetery was immensely sad; I didn't want to leave my sister behind. But being together made my pain easier.

When Max became ill, our daughter, Esther, came to be with him, staying in the hospital with him for two and a half months, sleeping on chairs. She would not leave to go back to her job until he was a little better. And our son stayed with me every night to help me when Max came home from the hospital, since we did not have help at night.

Even though Max was terribly ill, he never complained. The nurses and hospital workers adored him; one nurse came in when she was off duty just to wash his hair. Though he was weak, he wanted to write a letter to the editor of the Montreal *Gazette* to praise the people and their efforts to assist him. He did not have the strength to compose this letter, so he dictated it to Esther.

For thirty-eight years I went to sleep lying on his shoulder, and he comforted me. Even today, before going to bed, I always say good-night to him, kiss his picture and tell him how much I miss him. There is emptiness in my heart, and in the hearts of our children. We miss him terribly. And I think of the dreams we had, the plans we still had in mind for our future. I only wish that I had retired earlier – then we could have spent more time together, taking the train ride across Canada that he so dreamed of. Maybe one day I will take it myself in his memory. I will love him forever, and I miss him every day.

Glossary

aliyah (Hebrew; pl. *aliyot*, literally, ascent) A term used by Jews and modern Israelis to refer to Jewish immigration to Israel; the term is also used to refer to "going up" to the altar in a synagogue to read from the Torah.

American Jewish Joint Distribution Committee Also known colloquially as the "Joint." A charitable organization founded in 1914 to provide humanitarian assistance and relief to Jews all over the world in times of crisis. It provided material support for persecuted Jews in Germany and other Nazi-occupied territories and facilitated their immigration to neutral countries such as Portugal, Turkey and China. Between 1939 and 1944, JDC officials helped close to 81,000 European Jews find asylum in various parts of the world. Between 1944 and 1947, the JDC assisted more than 100,000 refugees living in DP camps by offering retraining programs, cultural activities and financial assistance for emigration.

antisemitism Prejudice, discrimination, persecution and/or hatred against Jewish people, institutions, culture and symbols.

Arrow Cross (in Hungarian, Nyilaskeresztes Párt – Hungarista Mozgalom; abbreviation: Nyilas) A Hungarian nationalistic and antisemitic party founded by Ferenc Szálasi in 1935 under the name the Party of National Will. With the full support of Nazi Germany, the newly renamed Arrow Cross Party ran in Hungary's 1939 election and won 25 per cent of the vote. The party was banned shortly after the elections but was legalized again in March 1944 when Germany occupied Hungary. Under Nazi approval, the party assumed control of Hungary from October 15, 1944, to March 1945, led by Szálasi under the name the Government of National Unity. The Arrow Cross regime was particularly brutal toward Jews – during their short period of rule between December 1944 and January 1945, approximately 20,000 Jews were murdered.

Auschwitz (German; in Polish, Oświęcim) A town in southern Poland approximately forty kilometres from Krakow, it is also the name of the largest complex of Nazi concentration camps that were built nearby. The Auschwitz complex contained three main camps: Auschwitz I, a slave labour camp built in May 1940; Auschwitz II-Birkenau, a death camp built in early 1942; and Auschwitz-Monowitz, a slave labour camp built in October 1942. In 1941, Auschwitz I was a testing site for usage of the lethal gas Zyklon B as a method of mass killing, which then went into wide usage. Between 1942 and 1944, transports arrived at Auschwitz-Birkenau from almost every country in Europe – hundreds of thousands from Poland, and thousands from France, the Netherlands, Greece, Slovakia, Bohemia and Moravia, Yugoslavia, Belgium, Italy and Norway. Between May 15 and July 8, 1944, approximately 435,000 Hungarian Jews were deported to Auschwitz. As well, more than 30,000 people were deported there from other concentration camps. It is estimated that 1.1 million people were murdered in Auschwitz; approximately 950,000 were Jewish; 74,000 Polish; 21,000 Roma; 15,000 Soviet prisoners of war; and 10,000–15,000 other nationalities. The Auschwitz complex was liberated by the Soviet army in January 1945.

Blockälteste (also *Blockältester*; German; literally, block elder) Prisoner appointed by the German authorities as barracks supervisor, charged with maintaining order and accorded certain privileges.

bris (Yiddish; in Hebrew, *brit milah*; literally, covenant of circumcision) Judaism's religious ceremony to welcome male infants into the covenant between God and the Children of Israel through a ritual circumcision (removal of the foreskin of the penis) performed by a mohel, or circumciser, eight days after the baby is born. The *kvatter* (German; messenger) takes the baby from his mother and brings him to where the circumcision will be performed. Traditionally, a baby boy is named after his bris.

Chanukah (also Hanukah; Hebrew; dedication) An eight-day festival celebrated in December to mark the victory of the Jews against foreign conquerors who desecrated the Temple in Jerusalem in the second century B C E. Traditionally, each night of the festival is marked by lighting an eight-branch candelabrum called a menorah to commemorate the rededication of the Temple and the miracle of its lamp burning for eight days with one day's worth of oil.

cholent (Yiddish) A traditional Jewish slow-cooked pot stew usually eaten as the main course at the festive Shabbat lunch on Saturdays after the synagogue service and on other Jewish holidays. For Jews of Eastern-European descent, the basic ingredients of *cholent* are meat, potatoes, beans and barley.

chuppah (Hebrew; literally, covering) The canopy used in traditional Jewish weddings that is usually made of a cloth (sometimes a prayer shawl) stretched or supported over four poles. It is meant to symbolize the home the couple will build together.

displaced persons (DPs) People who find themselves homeless and stateless at the end of a war. Following World War II, millions of people, especially European Jews, found that they had no homes to return to or that it was unsafe to do so. To resolve the staggering refugee crisis that resulted, Allied authorities and the United Nations Relief and Rehabilitation Administration (U N R R A) established Displaced Persons (DP) camps to provide temporary shelter and assistance to refugees, and help them transition toward resettlement. *See also* DP camps.

DP camps Facilities set up by the Allied authorities and the United Nations Relief and Rehabilitation Administration (UNRRA) in October 1945 to resolve the refugee crisis that arose at the end of World War II. The camps provided temporary shelter and assistance to the millions of people – not only Jews – who had been displaced from their home countries as a result of the war and helped them prepare for resettlement. *See also* United Nations Relief and Rehabilitation Administration (UNRRA).

gabba'im (plural of *gabbai*; Hebrew, tax collector) Historically, community officials who collected charity on behalf of the needy. Today, the term more commonly refers to a person with a high level of knowledge in Judaism who plays an important role in helping to lead synagogue services.

ghetto A confined residential area for Jews. The term originated in Venice, Italy, in 1516 with a law requiring all Jews to live on a segregated, gated island known as Ghetto Nuovo. Throughout the Middle Ages in Europe, Jews were often forcibly confined to gated Jewish neighbourhoods. During the Holocaust, the Nazis forced Jews to live in crowded and unsanitary conditions in rundown districts of cities and towns.

Hasidic Judaism (from the Hebrew word *hasid*; literally, piety) An Orthodox Jewish spiritual movement founded by Rabbi Israel ben Eliezer in eighteenth-century Poland, characterized by philosophies of mysticism and focusing on joyful prayer. This movement resulted in a new kind of leader who attracted disciples as opposed to the traditional rabbis who focused on the intellectual study of Jewish law. Melody and dance have an important role in Hasidic worship. There are many different sects of Hasidic Judaism, but followers of Hasidism often wear dark, conservative clothes as well as a head covering to reflect modesty and show respect to God.

High Holidays (also High Holy Days) The autumn holidays that mark the beginning of the Jewish year and that include Rosh

Hashanah (New Year) and Yom Kippur (Day of Atonement). Rosh Hashanah is observed with synagogue services where the leader of the service blows the shofar (ram's horn), and festive meals where sweet foods, such as apples and honey, are eaten to symbolize and celebrate a sweet new year. Yom Kippur, a day of fasting and prayer at synagogue, follows ten days later. *See also* Rosh Hashanah; Yom Kippur.

Hungarian Revolution (1956) A spontaneous uprising against the Soviet-backed Communist government of Hungary in October 1956, the Hungarian Revolution led to the brief establishment of a reformist government under Prime Minister Imre Nagy. The revolution was swiftly crushed by the Soviet invasion of November 1956, during which thousands of civilians were killed.

Iron Guard A fascist party founded in 1927, later known as the Legion or the Legionary Movement, that was based on Romanian nationalism and antisemitism. Its political influence spanned from 1930 to 1941, at which point it was crushed by the prime minister of Romania, Ion Antonescu.

kapo (German) A concentration camp prisoner appointed by the SS to oversee other prisoners as slave labourers.

kiddush (Hebrew; literally, sanctification) The blessing over wine that is recited on Shabbat and other Jewish holidays. *See also* Shabbat.

Labour Service (in Hungarian, *Munkaszolgálat*) Hungary's military-related labour service system, which was first established in 1919 for those considered too "politically unreliable" for regular military service. After the labour service was made compulsory in 1939, Jewish men of military age were recruited to serve; however, having been deemed "unfit" to bear arms, they were equipped with tools and employed in mining, road and rail construction and maintenance work. Though the men were treated relatively well at first, the system became increasingly punitive in nature. By 1941, Jews in forced labour battalions were required to wear a yellow armband and civilian clothes; they had no formal rank

and were unarmed; they were often mistreated by extremely antisemitic supervisors; and their work included clearing minefields,
causing their death. Between 20,000 and 40,000 Jewish men died
during their forced labour service.

Lagerälteste (German; literally, camp elder) A camp inmate in charge
of the prisoner population who reported to the SS *Rapportführer*
(Report Leader).

Markkleeberg A town in the Leipzig district of Germany where an
aircraft factory – the Junkers Flugzeug- und Motorenwerke AG
(Junkers Aircraft and Engine Company) – opened a munitions
plant in October 1943. Initially set up to house foreign forced labourers and workers from Germany, the facility became a forced
labour camp for women after an Allied bombing raid damaged
much of the original camp in February 1944. From August to December 1944, three transports of Hungarian-Jewish women arrived at the camp to perform heavy, demanding physical labour.
At its height, the camp held 1,539 Hungarian-Jewish inmates and
French political prisoners. Evacuated on April 13, 1945, the wom-
en were forced on a gruelling death march toward the Theresienstadt camp – approximately 700 women arrived at Theresienstadt
between April 30 and May 4, 1945; others had escaped en route
and were liberated by the Red Army, or had died either from the
harsh conditions or at the hands of the SS.

Mittelsteine A German forced labour camp in Lower Silesia that
mainly operated between August 1944 and April 1945. The camp
held between 300 to 1,000 Jewish women from Poland, Hungary
and Czechoslovakia who worked for a munitions manufacturer,
producing parts for V-1 and V-2 rockets. In March and April
1945, the camp was evacuated and the women were transferred
to various subcamps of the Gross-Rosen concentration camp –
Grafenort, Altheide and Mährisch Weisswasser.

Orthodox Judaism The set of beliefs and practices of Jews for whom
the observance of Jewish law is closely connected to faith; it is

characterized by strict religious observance of Jewish dietary laws, restrictions on work on the Sabbath and holidays, and a code of modesty in dress.

Passover One of the major festivals of the Jewish calendar, Passover takes place over eight days in the spring. Passover commemorates the liberation and exodus of the Israelite slaves from Egypt during the reign of the Pharaoh Ramses II. The festival begins with a lavish ritual meal called a seder, during which the story of Exodus is retold through the reading of a Jewish religious text called the Haggadah. With its special foods, songs and customs, the seder is the focal point of the Passover celebration and is traditionally a time of family gathering. The name of the festival refers to the fact that God "passed over" the houses of the Jews when he set about slaying the firstborn sons of Egypt as the last of the ten plagues aimed at convincing Pharaoh to free the Jews.

pogrom (Russian; to wreak havoc, to demolish) A violent attack on a distinct ethnic group. The term most commonly refers to nineteenth- and twentieth-century attacks on Jews in the Russian Empire.

Purim (Hebrew; literally, lottery) The celebration of the Jews' escape from annihilation in Persia. The Purim story, as told in the biblical Book of Esther, recounts how Haman, advisor to the King of Persia, planned to rid Persia of Jews, and how Queen Esther and her cousin Mordecai foiled Haman's plot by convincing the king to save the Jews. During the Purim festivities, people dress up as one of the figures in the Purim story; hold parades and retell the story of Haman, Esther and Mordecai; and give gifts of food to their friends and those in need.

Rosh Hashanah (Hebrew; literally, head of the year) The autumn holiday that marks the beginning of the Jewish year and ushers in the High Holy Days. It is observed by a synagogue service that ends with blowing the *shofar* (ram's horn), which marks the beginning of the holiday. The service is usually followed by a family dinner where sweet foods, such as apples and honey, are eaten to symbolize and celebrate a sweet new year. *See also* Yom Kippur.

Shabbat (Hebrew; in Yiddish, Shabbes, Shabbos) The weekly day of rest beginning Friday at sunset and ending Saturday at nightfall, ushered in by the lighting of candles on Friday evening and the recitation of blessings over wine and challah (egg bread); a day of celebration as well as prayer, it is customary to eat three festive meals, attend synagogue services and refrain from doing any work or travelling.

Shavuos (Hebrew; weeks) A Jewish festival celebrating the giving of the Ten Commandments at Mount Sinai, it occurs seven weeks after the first Passover seder. *See also* Passover.

SS (abbreviation of Schutzstaffel; Defence Corps). The SS was established in 1925 as Adolf Hitler's elite corps of personal bodyguards. Under the direction of Heinrich Himmler, its membership grew from 280 in 1929 to 50,000 when the Nazis came to power in 1933, and to nearly a quarter of a million on the eve of World War II. The SS was comprised of the Allgemeine-SS (General SS) and the Waffen-SS (Armed, or Combat SS). The General SS dealt with policing and the enforcement of Nazi racial policies in Germany and the Nazi-occupied countries. An important unit within the SS was the Reichssicherheitshauptamt (RSHA, the Central Office of Reich Security), whose responsibility included the Gestapo (Geheime Staatspolizei). The SS ran the concentration and death camps, with all their associated economic enterprises, and also fielded its own Waffen-SS military divisions, including some recruited from the occupied countries.

Stubenälteste (German; room elder) A senior prisoner who was in charge of a concentration camp barrack, under the command of a *Blockälteste. See also Blockälteste.*

Treaty of Trianon One of the five treaties produced at the 1919 Paris Peace Conference organized by the victors of World War I. The Treaty of Trianon imposed a harsh peace on Hungary, exacting reparations and redrawing its borders so that Hungary lost over two-thirds of its territory and about two-thirds of its inhabitants.

United Nations Relief and Rehabilitation Administration (UNRRA) An international relief agency created at a 44-nation conference in Washington, DC, on November 9, 1943, to provide economic assistance and basic necessities to war refugees. It was especially active in repatriating and assisting refugees in the formerly Nazi-occupied European nations immediately after World War II.

Vizhnitzer A rabbinic dynasty that began in the town of Vyzhnytsia, Poland (now Ukraine), with Menachem Mendel Hager (1830– 1884), the first Vizhnitzer rabbi. His great-grandson, Chaim Meir Hager (1888–1972), who became the fourth Vizhnitzer rabbi, survived World War II in Romania and settled in Israel in 1950, creating a religious community there.

yellow star A badge or armband with the Star of David on it that Jews in Nazi-occupied areas were frequently forced to wear as an identifying mark of their lesser status and to single them out as targets for persecution. The six-pointed Star of David is the ancient and most recognizable symbol of Judaism.

Yiddish A language derived from Middle High German with elements of Hebrew, Aramaic, Romance and Slavic languages, and written in Hebrew characters. Spoken by Jews in east-central Europe for roughly a thousand years from the tenth century to the mid-twentieth century, it was still the most common language among European Jews until the outbreak of World War II. There are similarities between Yiddish and contemporary German.

Yom Kippur (Hebrew; literally, Day of Atonement) A solemn day of fasting and repentance that comes eight days after Rosh Hashanah, the Jewish New Year, and marks the end of the high holidays. *See also* Rosh Hashanah.

Photographs:
Zsuzsanna Fischer Spiro

1   2

3

1   Zsuzsanna's paternal grandfather, Elias, with her father, Ervin, and her uncles, Laszlo and Miklos. Kisvárda, circa 1900.

2   Gizella (Funk) Fischer, Zsuzsanna's mother, date unknown.

3   Ten-year-old Zsuzsanna (third from left) with her brothers, Endre (far left) and Tibor, and her older sister, Klara. Tornyospálca, circa 1935.

1 The Fischer family before the war. Standing in back, left to right: Klara, Endre, Tibor and Zsuzsanna. In front: their mother, Gizella, and their father, Ervin. Kisvárda, 1942.

2 Zsuzsanna (far left), Tibor and Klara, with their father, Ervin, after the war.

1

2

3

1 Zsuzsanna in Kisvárda, 1946.
2 In Budapest, 1949.
3 The diary that Zsuzsanna began writing in Leipzig, Germany, 1945.

1 Wedding photo of Zsuzsanna (Susan) and Józsi (Joseph) Spiro. Budapest, September 11, 1949.

2 Zsuzsanna and Józsi, 1983.

1 Zsuzsanna with a candleholder from the former Kisvárda synagogue.
2 Zsuzsanna and Józsi, 2010.

1   With her children and grandchildren, 2013. In back, left to right: Jason; Eli; daughter-in-law Frances; and sons Peter and David. In front, left to right: Zsuzsanna; Hannah; daughter-in-law Rachel with Shoshana; Devorah; Jacob; and Ariel.

2   At the 2014 Sustaining Memories celebration with volunteer writing partner Fran Weisman (far left), and Zsuzsanna's grandchildren Ariel, Devorah, Jacob, Shoshana and Hannah.

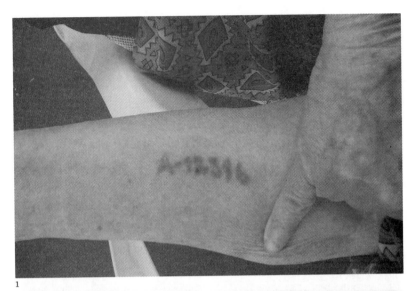

1

2

1   Zsuzsanna showing the number she was tattooed with at Auschwitz-Birkenau.
2   At the candle-lighting commemoration on Holocaust Remembrance Day, 2015.

Photographs: Eva Shainblum

1 Dora and David Rosenberg, Eva's maternal grandparents, circa 1922.
2 Eva's mother, Esther (far left) with her parents, Dora and David (centre), and siblings. Halmi, Hungary, 1922.

1   Wedding photo of Eva's parents, Esther and Béla Steinberger. Halmi, 1923.
2   Eva's siblings Ella and Paul. Nagyvárad, 1927.
3   The Steinberger family, circa 1933. From left to right: Eva's mother, Esther, Reizi
    (Eva), Paul, David, Ella and Eva's father, Béla.

Eva and her sister, Ella, wearing the watches given to them by their parents. Nagyvárad, 1943.

1 Eva (right) and her friend Adele in Oradea, 1946.
2 Eva (left) and her cousin Zsofi. Germany, 1946.
3 Eva and her boyfriend, Tibi Goldberger, in 1946.

1   Eva and Max Shainblum on their engagement day, 1959.

2   Celebrating their wedding on September 24, 1959.

3   Max and Eva with their son, Mark, and daughter, Esther, 1982.

4   Esther and Mark at a friend's wedding, 1989.

Eva's aunt Lenke and her husband, Moritz.

1

2

3

1 Eva at the gravestone of her sister, Ella. Oradea, 1992.

2 Max and Eva outside her former home in Oradea, 1992.

3 The Shainblum family, 1997.

1 Eva's daughter, Esther, with her husband, Irv.
2 Eva's son, Mark, with his wife, Andrea.
3 Eva's granddaughter Maya Gabriella, 2008.
4 Eva and her granddaughter Noa Michaela, 2014.

Index

The Azrieli Foundation was established in 1989 to realize and extend the philanthropic vision of David J. Azrieli, C.M., C.Q., M.Arch. The Foundation's mission is to support a wide spectrum of initiatives in education and research. The Azrieli Foundation is an active supporter of programs in the fields of Education, the education of architects, scientific and medical research, and the arts. The Azrieli Foundation's many initiatives include: the Holocaust Survivor Memoirs Program, which collects, preserves, publishes and distributes the written memoirs of survivors in Canada; the Azrieli Institute for Educational Empowerment, an innovative program successfully working to keep at-risk youth in school; the Azrieli Fellows Program, which promotes academic excellence and leadership on the graduate level at Israeli universities; the Azrieli Music Project, which celebrates and fosters the creation of high-quality new Jewish orchestral music; and the Azrieli Neurodevelopmental Research Program, which supports advanced research on neurodevelopmental disorders, particularly Fragile X and Autism Spectrum Disorders.